WILD THINGS

WILD THINGS

MIKE CAPUZZO

FAWCETT COLUMBINE

NEW YORK

A Fawcett Columbine Book
Published by Ballantine Books
Copyright © 1995 by Mike Capuzzo

All rights reserved under International and Pan-American Copyright Conventions. Published in the United States by Ballantine Books, a division of Random House, Inc., New York, and simultaneously in Canada by Random House of Canada Limited, Toronto. The contents of this work were previously published in different form as columns in various newspapers.

Library of Congress Catalog Card Number: 94-94574

ISBN: 0-449-90895-X

Cover design by Judy Herbstman
Cover illustration by Bonnie Timmons
Text design by Debby Jay

Manufactured in the United States of America
First Edition: February 1995
10 9 8 7 6 5 4 3 2 1

To Jill, Grace, Julia, Daisy,
Buddy, and ol' Blue

CONTENTS

ACKNOWLEDGMENTS

First, I want to assure you that *Wild Things* has been factory-tested to provide years of gentle laughter easily muffled by running water or a fully closed bathroom door. But, and I swear it is no fault of the author, you will also find shining within these apparent humor columns the fire of crusaders and the love of saints. Yes, all mistakes and distortions are mine, but the passion, humanity, and dedication toward living things must be blamed entirely on the following:

Rachel Lamb, director of companion animals at the Humane Society of the United States in Washington, D.C., whose surpassing knowledge and compassion for critters makes the capital a more humane place; master dog trainers and authors Brian Kilcommons and Sarah Wilson, whose genius with dogs is based on remarkable intuition and compassion for people. Roger Caras, storyteller nonpareil, who showed me that angels exist and are hard at work protecting the animal kingdom. Edward O. Wilson, "the Father of Biodiversity," who taught me the cosmic importance of every ant and, by extension, every piebald mutt. *Wild Things* would not exist without the keen insights and unflagging support of Diana Loevy, the impre-

ACKNOWLEDGMENTS

sario of United Feature Syndicate; the editing talents and animal humor of Kirk Nicewonger; the faith and wisdom under pressure of Sherri Rifkin of Ballantine Books.

And, finally, a round of appreciation for David Vigliano, Steve Sonsky, Lorraine Branham (a true leader at the *Philadelphia Inquirer*), Teresa Banik (whose research informs much of this book), Lisa Wilson, Maryanne Grimes, Bruce Boynick, Christopher Boyd, David O'Reilly, Mary South, and Joel Achenbach, the wonderful *Washington Post* columnist and author, who said during a pickup basketball game: "You really have to write this column about animals. People love animals. People will read it."

INTRODUCTION

The idea for *Wild Things* came to me in a dream. This is not exactly true, but I owe it to the many people who believed in me as a "new journalist," primarily concerned with important human stories in narrative form, to start this way. Now I am a "meow journalist," primarily concerned with cats, dogs, and other critters. Here's how it happened:

The idea for *Wild Things* came to me when I was interviewing His Excellency the President of Argentina, Carlos Menem. There we were, propped up on Louis XIV–style red velvet chairs in a private suite at the Plaza Hotel in New York, the Latin American specialists from the *New York Times*, *Time* magazine, *U.S. News & World Report*, and me, representing the *Philadelphia Inquirer*.

Time was grilling Menem on Argentina's runaway inflation, and I, as an award-winning Serious Journalist, was mulling a question on the president's forthcoming historic speech to the United Nations when it occurred to me that the question readers really care about is, "Where does kitty litter come from?"

I diplomatically bit my tongue, but *Wild Things* was a-borning. Another inspiration was from one of the great newspaper editors of our time, who once said, and I paraphrase, "As long as I am editor of this great newspaper, we will never run a pet obituary!" You can look it up.

Intuitively, you'll pardon the expression, I knew this was donkey-backwards. Like you, I believe newspapers should devote entire sections to animals because (a) Americans spend $20 billion a year on their pets and only $15 billion on movies and videos; (b) grandparents spend more money on their pets than on their grandchildren; and (c) most spouses prefer the company of their dogs and cats to their spouses. This is all true.

Another crucial event in the development of *Wild Things* occurred at 1:17 P.M. on July 3, 1987, as I was walking my new dog, Blue, in a park west of 25th and Pine streets in Philadelphia. Presently, I encountered Another Man Walking His Dog, and entered into the following conversation:

ME: "What kind of dog is that? He's beautiful."

ANOTHER MAN WALKING HIS DOG: "He's a Bichon Frise, a great favorite of the French and Italian nobility. And your dog is—?"

ME: "We're not sure. We think he's got some Lab in him, but—"

ANOTHER MAN WALKING HIS DOG: "Oh, he's only a mutt."

This comment touched me with those two time-honored emotions heralded by all the Western poets, namely *confusion* and *shame*. After years of research, I now know that my dog Blue is one of the most hardy and popular types in the United States, the Black Dog. In response, I led a national campaign urging President Clinton to cease his foolish attempts to buy a purebred golden retriever and *adopt a mutt*. But I'm getting ahead of the story.

If you own one of the 250 million pet cats, dogs, horses, birds, hamsters, skunks, or reticulated pythons in America, admire the beasts in the zoo, or fear for the rhinos in Africa, *Wild Things* is for you.

But first, a statement of philosophy.

The Darwin of our time, Edward O. Wilson of Harvard University, believes "our existence depends" on the human bond with other species: "our spirit is woven from it, hope rises on its currents."

The Tolstoy of our time, Milan Kundera, writes in *The Unbearable Lightness of Being*: "No one can give anyone else the gift of the idyll; only an animal can do so, because only animals were not expelled from Paradise. The love between dog and man is idyllic." In the final chapter of *The Unbearable Lightness of Being*, doomed lovers Tomas and Tereza measure their sweet last days through their dying dog.

The Pet Column of our time, "Wild Things" stands for these things and many other profound questions, such as, "If cats are miniature African lions, why don't they eat us when we sleep?" Yes, we believe there is nothing more important to your health, your emotional well-being, and the fate of the planet than the animals in your life.

Finally, I'd like to introduce one of the millions of readers of the "Wild Things" column, Mrs. Phyllis Rubenstein of North Miami, Florida. Phyllis wrote me a nine-page letter remembering her shepherd mix, Nandie, whom she rescued from an abusive neighbor in 1972. Phyllis—whose "present inventory" includes six cats, a female mix dog, and a three-year-old female North American skunk, Petunia II—bought a house with a yard primarily so Nandie could enjoy the fenced spaces.

"Dear Mike," Phyllis wrote. "As the years progressed she lost her hearing and her legs began to give. She had a difficult time . . . on the terrazzo floors and I laid small rugs in a path for her . . . doggie boots, red rubber ones, worked for a time. . . . I fixed a ramp because she couldn't handle the steps to the yard. Finally the day came when she could no longer stand and I carried her out to her beloved back-yard. . . . She looked at me with those big, beautiful brown eyes clouded by age . . . Mike, I had had this old gal for nineteen and a half years, and I think she was telling me it was time. . . . Writing this had been a catharsis and I thank you for that. . . ."

Wild Things offers expert tips on many things, such as coping with the loss of a pet. If you can't do it on your own, try the Pet Loss Support Helpline sponsored by the Chicago Veterinary Medical Association, at (708) 603-3994; or the Pet Loss Hotline at the Center for Animals in Society at the University of California at Davis, (916) 752-4200. Consultation is free, except for long-distance charges, and callers are allowed to "get permission" to feel grief for dying and deceased pets, says Bonnie Mader, director of the Davis hotline.

You don't, however, need permission to adore animals. Just read *Wild Things*, and enjoy the unbeatable fun of owning or observing an animal. And send me your letters, your stories (especially the uproarious ones), your photographs, and your pet obits. I'll print them in my column, to be shown in many of our great newspapers.

WILD THINGS

CHAPTER 1

LOVE & SEX THINGS

INCLUDING THE SEXUAL KING OF BEASTS,

THE FOUR-YEAR ITCH,

WHY CONGRESSMEN BEHAVE LIKE CHIMPANZEES,

AND WHY PASSION FADES IN MICE AND MEN

How Can Dogs and Cats Improve One's Love Life?

A very important feature not explained in the User's Manual for your pet is: how to attract single females and males or whatever wild thing you desire on Valentine's Day. If you've already discussed all the great books and worn the treads off the Stairmaster and you're still waking up to the sad choking gurgles of a one-cup espresso machine, these are the three most important words you will ever read (with the possible exception of REGISTER TO VOTE, although we doubt it because democracy cannot survive with a *declining birthrate*).

Get a dog. The wonderful thing about owning a dog, aside from having to buy paper towels all the time, is you can effortlessly *meet beautiful women.* Or attract men, whatever your pleasure. And not just anybody. Just the right person for you, as determined by your dog, who is a superb judge of character.

Dog lovers have known this for years. "The best way to meet somebody is to walk your dog down the street," said dog trainer Sarah Wilson, coauthor of *Good Owners, Great Dogs.* "You automatically become kinder, more trustworthy, a better person if you're with a dog." Women who are intimidated by talking to a strange man will warm up easily to a man walking a dog, giving you the benefit of numerous superb qualities, many of which you don't even have. "Nice dog," as icebreakers go, sounds far more acceptable and sincere than the lines that worked perfectly to keep me unattached for years: "Nice day, huh?" or "I didn't think it was supposed to rain." (Mutts adopted from the pound, of course, work best to melt hearts.)

When you adopt a dog, "you immediately and effortlessly become a member of the club," Wilson said. "You join a society, and you meet people that way." You join the late-afternoon walk to your local Dog Hill or Dog Park, where bankers, computer programmers, plumbers, lawyers, and defendants all hang out in one of the last great truly democratic associations, the Dog People Club.

"Then you break off and go for a walk with two or three friends," Wilson said. "It's a great way to get to know someone without any pressure." When you do meet someone, your dog becomes even more important, as the final arbiter of this suitor's character. "I always trust my dog's opinion," Wilson said. "And I know a lot of women who do the same. If my dog doesn't like someone, he'll back away from being petted, or stand quietly by me, eyeing the person. Time and again, the dog has been right."

Cats, too, can serve valuable romantic purposes. Peter Gethers, best-selling author of *The Cat Who Went to Paris*, carries Norton, his Scottish Fold, around the world, often in his arms. "Women think I'm more sensitive, a nicer guy," he told me. "The best way to meet beautiful women is to carry a cat."

How Long Does Marriage Last?

Four years. And you thought it was a "seven-year itch." The truth is worse, according to anthropologist Helen Fisher. She studied divorce records in more than forty countries and sixty societies since 1947, and discovered a striking pattern. "It's a four-year itch," Fisher says.

In her book *Anatomy of Love*, Fisher theorizes that the first "marriages" among our prehuman ancestors went splitsville after four years—and life hasn't changed in millions of years. "Picture our first pair-bonded couple, male and female," Fisher says. "They have a child, and when the child is an infant there is a powerful need for the couple to stay together for the child's survival. But when the child is about four, old enough to be watched by other adults and older children in ancient 'play-groups,' " Fisher says, the male (hunter) goes over the hill and mates again. As does the female (gatherer).

Such breakups are the rule in the animal kingdom. Ninety percent of birds make pair-bonds, but after the chicks leave the nest, then it's off to divorce court. Young chicks, Fisher says, "always fly off to a male who has a bigger, more attractive nest. For . . . years, women have been attracted to older men because they have more resources," Fisher says. "And older man have been drawn to younger women because they have fresher eggs."

Why Did an Internationally Known Composer Give His Heart to a Dog?

This is the story of Martin, a man who gave up his job and friends and built a ramp in front of his house to care for the love of his life, who was ailing so much that it broke Martin's heart. Martin was only in his thirties when his beloved Maya began to falter, so he had to carry her everywhere and feed her by hand. Ah, but they had shared such fine times together, Martin and Maya. And these last years—riding through summer evenings to the Dairy Queen, Maya closing her eyes and feeling the breeze in her hair—these were the sweetest moments of all.

Neighbors thought Martin Scot Kosins, a successful composer, had broken his leg, or built the ramp for an ailing grandmother in a wheelchair. Neighbors were wrong. Martin, an internationally known composer-pianist, built the ramp to care for his elderly dog, Maya.

Martin's extraordinary devotion to Maya is the subject of a book, *Maya's First Rose: Diary of a Very Special Love*, which speaks to everyone who has loved and lost a pet.

Martin didn't even want the shepherd-boxer-you-guess-the-rest puppy he took home from a pet shop more than twenty years ago. His wife insisted on a dog. Five years later, the wife left; Maya stayed.

As a puppy, Maya sat under the piano bench listening as Martin composed for artists such as Sir Neville Marriner and Bud Shank, as he produced songs by John Carradine,

Loretta Swit, and the Ink Spots. Maya thrilled to the music, and when Martin left she sat by the window awaiting his return. Maya, Martin says, "was God's gift to the beauty of my life."

Martin was devastated when, at age ten, Maya's back legs began to stiffen from age. She underwent an operation, which was followed by casts on her legs. When Maya became too weak to climb stairs, Martin built the ramp to their house. To care for her enlarged heart and weak lungs he fed her, by hand, a special diet of boiled hamburger and low-salt kibble. At fifteen, Maya suffered a stroke and Martin gave up his traveling career as a musician, vowing never to leave her side again.

For two years he put aside work, family, and friends, who thought he was crazy. "Just put her away," they said. "Don't be a damn fool." But Maya, though ailing, was not in pain, her veterinarian assured Martin. Yes, the old girl had quality of life. Dinner with friends had to be near Martin's house so he could be back for Maya within two hours. "No movie," he says, "was that important." Martin found a grocery store that delivered. He took his phone calls and read his mail next to her. On their last night together, a few days before Christmas 1988, Martin wrapped Maya in the pea coat he had worn during their years together, cradled her in his lap, and sang until her last breath.

That New Year's Eve, Martin began to write. He wrote for himself and he wrote for all the people who were ashamed at the depth of their feelings about losing an animal. "If your experience is similar to mine," Kosins, now forty-six, says, "you may find yourself constantly occupied with thoughts of your late pet. . . . You must talk to someone. Do not hide your feelings because most people will think 'It was only a pet.' "

How Can I Find the Right Mate in the Animal Kingdom?

Many readers of the "Wild Things" column are seeking advice on making a lasting love connection. Who do we look like, Ann Landers? Instead, we called Helen Fisher at the American Museum of Natural History in New York. Fisher is a worthy sage on human mating practices, since she is an expert on chimpanzees. I spent several hours with Fisher sipping Italian coffees in a café where men and women were madly preening themselves like a flock of sex-crazed birds. At one point I told Fisher that my daughter was three years old and she said glumly, "I'm sorry,"— three being the age when most animals leave their young to spread their seed according to Darwinian principles they can't control.

Here, with help from Helen Fisher, is the "Wild Things" guide to courting and mating based on what *really works* among the animals, who taught us everything we know about wild sex.

Flirting is the traditional way men demonstrate their obvious charm and desirability to a member of the opposite sex by leaning against the bar puffing their chests out like baboons on the grasslands of eastern Africa.

Women begin flirting by flaunting certain curves like chimpanzees—who simply bend over. (Catherine de Médicis introduced High Chimpanzee Style to European fashion in the 1500s when she invented the high-heeled shoe, which arches the back and tilts the buttocks suggestively.) According to Fisher, all of our preening, courting, and flirting gestures are a legacy of our animal past.

Once you've *gotten his/her attention*, the next step is to say something highly impressive such as "Been here before?" True, this is completely witless—but so are all pickup lines, even those employed by the "lower" animals, who use nonsensical "grooming talk" to break the ice, the behaviorist Desmond Morris notes.

If you receive a lilting, singsongy reply and an open or "high" smile, with upper gums exposed, it could be your lucky day. *Warning:* If, instead, you get a curt response or actual bared teeth, this is gorilla, chimp, and California Valley Girl body language for "Get lost or I'll start shooting." Move on to another mammal.

If you're getting happy, gum-heavy smiles, proceed cautiously to the *courting* phase, the first step of which is the *dinner date*. The dinner date is the way respectable men in our society invite women to a romantic restaurant for a lovely, civilized dining experience, with expensive Bordeaux, tiramisu, and the full expectation of wanton sexual favors in return. Offering food in exchange for sex is the most common ploy in the animal kingdom. Yes, as one of our famous anthropologists says, "The estrous female consumes the (food) gift, then copulates with the donor." It's one of the guy-rules of nature. For instance, when the black-tipped hang fly catches a juicy daddy longlegs, he secretes an abdominal scent that attracts a female hang fly, who stops to enjoy the meal, then copulates.

If your date is not behaving like a fly or roadrunner (whose females are highly excited by a little lizard snack), encourage *synchronicity*. You sip your almond decaf mochachino. She sips her almond decaf mochachino. You cross your legs. She crosses her legs. These are highly encouraging signs. Chimps, too, mirror each other's movements by swaying from side to side just prior to copulation.

If you're on to the Frangelico and your date still isn't employing a *singsongy voice* or *synchronicity*, go for it anyway.

Species that survive don't waffle. Yes, it's time for the deal-clincher, what anthropologists call the *copulatory gaze*. Chimps and other primates do this, and you must, too, if you are to achieve true love, or at least that highest principle of Darwinian thought, random sex. An impressive role-model *copulatory gazer* was a baboon named Alex who stared wantonly fifteen feet across a room at a female baboon named Thalia, who gave him the all-important *return gaze*. Whereupon Alex "flattened his ears against his head, narrowed his eyelids and began to smack his lips," Fisher said. Encouraged by intense *return gazing*, Alex made his approach and received supplicant grooming from Thalia, "the beginning of a . . . sexual liaison that was still going strong six years later," Fisher writes.

Caution to male primates: Proceed slowly. Don't lean too close, talk too much, touch too soon. Courting among humans, wolf spiders, baboons, and other creatures involves passing a series of tests, proceeding cautiously. One goof and it's curtains on the whole show, and remember, in all species, *it's her show.* The male wolf spider, for instance, must enter the long, dark foyer of the female's dwelling to court and copulate. This he does *very* slowly. If he seems overeager, she devours him. That's life.

Why Are Lions the "Kings of Sexual Beasts"?

No wonder kings put lions on their coats of arms. Aside from unmatched size, strength, and courage, lions sport a sex life that makes the Marquis de Sade's sound tame. The huge male, the so-called King of Beasts, mounts the female from behind and *seizes her neck in his jaws*, which sometimes draws blood and *excites* both of them. S&M is a regular stimulant in the sex lives of animals. During copulation, the big male cat's mighty meows can be heard across the plains, and the female makes a continuous low growl, both of them baring their teeth. This lasts a minute tops, possibly only six seconds. The mighty male lets out a drawn-out *YOWL!* as he ejaculates, then quickly dismounts. Then they lie entangled and spent in their bed, smoking and looking out on the neon lights of the city, and doing it again . . . and again. One male was observed by researchers copulating with two females 155 times in fifty-five hours.

After the male finishes his impressive performance, he slumps to the ground exhausted and the insatiable female goes off looking for someone else. She copulates every fifteen minutes for several days, with no time out for normal pursuits, such as eating.

How Many Animals Are Monogamous?

When you remain monogamous, you are expressing one of the highest human ideals, one which is shared by approximately *four other creatures*, namely, the wood roach, the dung beetle, and several forms of lice. This is not counting the thousands of mammals, among whom a full *3 percent* practice monogamy, including the Asiatic clawless otter, deer mice, the klipspringer, siamangs, South American monkeys, all of the wild dogs, and the dik-dik, a very small antelope in Ethiopia that has never cheated on his wife. Yes, mammals (that's you, pal) have evolved a biological drive to behave like . . . Elizabeth Taylor! This is called *se-*

rial monogamy. "Lots of marriages and lots of affairs in between—that's our pattern over time throughout history," Fisher says.

Monogamy is rare in mammals, Fisher says, "because it is not normally the male's genetic advantage to remain with one female when he can copulate with several and pass on more of his genes to posterity."

Why Do Our Politicians Behave Like Chimpanzees?

What our most progressive schools fail to teach us is that the most noteworthy characteristic of human beings is that we are descended from chimpanzees, and *chimpanzees are highly intelligent creatures characterized by astonishing sexual energy; ergo, chimps are wildly promiscuous.* This is why politicians can't keep their pants on. It's anyone's guess how our prehuman ancestors bonded and courted, but if humans did indeed evolve from the apes, and if modern chimpanzees are a guide, these prehumans "lived in a community where everyone copulated with everyone," Helen Fisher says. *Remember:* We are genetically as similar to the chimp as the dog is to the wolf.

According to animal-sex researcher Susan Windybank, author of *Wild Sex: Way Beyond the Birds and the Bees*, "the female chimpanzee has an appetite for sex to rival the lioness and a sexual stamina to match. . . . Promiscuity is the byword of the chimpanzee's sexual life." Every month the chimps devote ten days to a gang bang in which males line up to copulate, very briefly, with a female. (One female was observed mating with eight different males in fifteen minutes.)

Why Is Homosexuality Common in Nature When It Doesn't Lead to Nature's Most Important Activity, Procreation?

Ah, but it does. Some primates and mammals, such as horses, cows, and dolphins, go through a homosexual phase as "practice," working on their flirting and other skills before they are sexually mature enough to attract a female. Practice makes perfect. Young male baboons, for instance, offer themselves sexually to dominant older male baboons in return for protection and favors.

In fact, some important scientists believe that every creature can trace its ancestry back to the common earthworm, including humans, as earthworms were the first jointed animal, an evolutionary breakthrough. And earthworms are born through a pure homosexual union.

"Wild Things" staffers are loath to judge lifestyles, but the oddest sexual habit we've heard of (though never witnessed) is homosexual slugs who engage in anal sex while suspended from their own slime. Let's *out* them right here and now: the European great grey slug and the American black slug. The slugs "wrap themselves around each other and throw themselves into the air with a rope of slime acting as a safety line," says Windybank in *Wild Sex*. "As they dangle from the slime both slugs whip out huge two-inch penises (half their body size) and wrap these around each other to exchange sperm." Later the sexual organs are put away, as they would make slug transportation impossible. "Which goes to show," Windybank says, "that length is not necessarily an advantage."

Why Does Sexual Attraction Feel So Powerful . . . and Then Fade Away?

Infatuation is a chocolate high—you grow addicted to it, and after a while, you come down. During infatuation, according to psychiatrist Michael Liebowitz, the neurons in the limbic system of the brain, our emotional core, are bathed in phenylethylamine (PEA). PEA is the magical stuff in chocolate bars, too. When mice are injected with PEA, they jump and squeal in exhilaration at first—what researchers call "popcorn behavior"—but, alas, even in mice that special someone starts to lose his animal appeal. Rhesus monkeys smack their lips suggestively under PEA's influence, and baboons press a lever 160 times in three hours to keep getting hits.

The speed-rush of these natural drugs can buoy a couple for two, even three years, particularly if barriers—like oceans or existing marriages—stand in their way. This is why lovers are so giddy, so full of life, some anthropologists believe.

Eventually, Liebowitz suggests, the brain can no longer endure the speed-high of PEA, of romantic bliss, and there is a measurable drop in levels of natural stimulants in the brain. If you're lucky, you will receive a second drug bath—the increased production of endorphins, the opiates of the mind, the chemical of long attachment. If, however, you yearn for that old, wild high with someone other than your spouse, we recommend *massive amounts of Godiva*.

Why Do Females Get the "Munchies" after Sex (i.e., Devour Their Mates)?

Talk about your man-eaters. The most famous sexual cannibal is the praying mantis, who does not wait for the sex act to end before beginning to eat her mate alive. Fortunately his sex drive is so strong the male praying mantis is able to continue having sex while being devoured.

Other females that share this cannibalistic compulsion are the scorpion, the tarantula, the wheel-web spider, and the ant lion, who devours her mate and proceeds to kill and eat all the males she can find. But why? "Often it's because of a condition known as protein hunger," Susan Windybank explains. "After the male has performed his function, fertilizing the female, he becomes superfluous and . . . would soon die anyway. Instead of wasting the wonderful nutrients in his body the female eats him. Thus, he acts as both father and food for the future offspring."

Why Can't the World's Largest Gorilla Get a Date?

Each year, particularly as fall turns to winter and warmth and light disappear from some parts of the world, "Wild Things" hastens to remind ambitious two-career couples and all stressed Americans that most experts recommend that all human beings would be happier if they had sex once a week.

Gorillas and chimpanzees, being our closest evolutionary cousins, are also happier if they're having regular intimate relations. I know what you're thinking: Given that chimps spend an inordinate amount of time swinging in trees and exploring as many other chimps as possible in what family newspapers call "the biblical way," this means the entire glorious human race is descended from promiscuous monkeys. This is true and explains not only the divorce rate in our society but the private lives of some of our United States congressmen, who, it has been scientifically shown, have nearly identical reproductive systems to African gorillas.

This also explains why the gorilla named Colossus, who is smart and sensitive and has never been mistaken for a congressman, was so sad. Colossus is a magnificent hunk of a gorilla, sort of the Fabio of lowland gorillas. But like Fabio, who told "Wild Things" in an interview that he is still looking for that special someone, it's Saturday night and Colossus ain't got nobody. Mighty Colossus is the largest lowland gorilla in captivity—six foot two and an impressive 575 pounds—twenty-eight years old and still a virgin. He spent twenty years in a small cage in New Hampshire without even *seeing* another female gorilla.

My friend Guillermo, a bachelor in Chicago, assures me that many single men can relate to this. Still, it would not only be fun for Colossus to have sex, it's downright important to the survival of his species. The African lowland gorilla is an endangered species, with fewer than twenty thousand remaining.

Zoos no longer take gorillas from the wild because of their dwindling numbers, so gorillas in zoos must be born and bred in zoos. This is problematic because there are only about 280 captive gorillas in zoos and their bloodlines can't be crossed or it's like cousins marrying cousins. Colossus was born in the wild and was unrelated to all other gorillas in captivity. No wonder, then, that zookeepers were thrilled when Colossus was rescued from his New

Hampshire cage and provided with a female gorilla love-mate in a zoo in Gulf Breeze, Florida.

"We'd love to get some genetic material from him," said zoo director Pat Quinn, which is a line Guillermo has been waiting for years to hear.

Alas, Colossus's love-mate, as chosen by the captive breeding program Computer Gorilla Dating Service, was a female who in some strange way embodied all the charms of her name: Muke. Muke was a healthy twenty-seven but had never shown the slightest interest in sex. She had, in fact, been a terror, a 275-pounder, big for a female, who liked to "knock the hell out of" males who crossed her path in the St. Louis Zoo. One zookeeper likened her to "an old Bronx housewife."

This was the first female gorilla Colossus had ever laid eyes on. He reached out gently to touch her hand. She bit him. He tried to hug her. She drew blood from his neck with a long scratch. They spent their early courtship throwing dung at each other.

Welcome to the fairer sex, big guy.

After more than four years of this—including many sperm counts taken from Colossus (don't ask how), the injection of human fertility drugs into both Muke and Colossus, and X-rated gorilla flicks—the Bickersons of the animal kingdom managed not to have sex. Not once. Colossus, 570 pounds, was too intimidated. Fabio no doubt would be too, of Muke. By the end Colossus couldn't take his eyes off a blonde secretary who visited the zoo often. The breakup was a major national story, which the always responsible Associated Press reported as SPLITSVILLE FOR HUGE GORILLA AND BIG GIRLFRIEND.

This past spring, Colossus was moved to the Cincinnati Zoo, where he was installed in a harem with six females, which is something Guillermo has been waiting his whole life to have happen. "Colossus is doing wonderfully, and he's usually on exhibit with four females," said zoo public relations director Barbara Rish. "He's such a draw to the public in Cincinnati, everybody thinks he's just a fantastic gorilla. If you ever saw him, he's incredible. He's just fantastic."

Colossus, alas, retains his virginity. "Our females still seem to be somewhat intimidated, and usually the female makes the advance," Rish said. "It may take a while."

As Guillermo likes to say, "It's worth the wait."

Four-Year Animal Itch: Shakespeare

1592: Three or four years after marrying, William Shakespeare inhales a peeled "love apple" a woman has kept under her armpit for nine and a half weeks, leaves wife, Anne, and twin daughters in Stratford to pursue writing career in London.

Four-Year Itch: Sarah Ferguson

1992: The four-year itch strikes the Duchess of York in an unusual place—her toes. Three to four years after her celebrated wedding to Prince Andrew, Ferguson is photographed letting a married American businessman lick between her toes, giving new meaning to the term "royal footman."

Four-Year Itch: Woody Allen

1992: A boy named Satchel reaches the evolutionarily vulnerable age of four years old, and his family breaks up. His father, Woody Allen, runs off with a younger female. Mia shows dominant behavior expected of the silverback male in a gorilla harem.

Four-Year Itch: Princes Charles

1993: Having fathered his Darwinian quota of two children with Princess Di, Prince Charles feels free to display his true feelings to Camilla Parker Bowles, showing his love of British architecture at the same time. "In the next life," he tells her, "I want to come back as the elastic on your foundational undergarments." Or something like that.

Four-Year Itch: Donald Trump

1994: After dumping Marla Maples an estimated 323 times in four years, Donald Trump begets daughter Tiffany and yields to evolutionary pressure to marry the mother and protect the helpless infant. Expressing his love of Marla by citing his fear of the Long Island Railroad massacre and the presence of sexually transmitted diseases in society, Trump takes a solemn vow to remain married, for at least four years.

Nature's Wildest Lover

The desert rat, Shaw's Jird, was observed copulating 224 times in two hours.

Sex with Dolphins Can Be Dangerous

The federal government is rather busy right now investigating suspected sexual contacts between humans and dolphins. A sharp-eyed reader sent us a clipping from the Philadelphia *Daily News*, which is a tabloid newspaper whose editors know that an X-rated video filmed in Key Largo, Florida, of a young woman frolicking with a dolphin is a matter of keen importance in its readers' lives. "The woman laughs and appears to exhibit no fear," the *Daily News* reports. "When she later tries to get out of the lagoon, the dolphin blocks her exit. . . . The dolphin becomes aroused and repeatedly [PORTION DELETED BY RESPONSIBLE EDITORS] against the woman."

Never swim with Flipper-type dolphins, who are very physical, sexually charged creatures who jump easily from homosexual to heterosexual encounters (thus the quaint nickname "Flipper"). This happens in group dolphin orgies in which the average person *should not participate*. "That Florida woman was lucky she wasn't hurt," a dolphin expert told "Wild Things."

CHAPTER 2

WHITE HOUSE
CAT THINGS

IN WHICH CATS TAKE OVER THE WHITE HOUSE,

A FIRST LADY DROWNS KITTENS,

AND SOCKS ATTEMPTS SUICIDE

Power Shifts from Millie to Socks

Many "Wild Things" friends and readers, ever alert to major animal-news trends, have noted with pleasure that the party long out of power has taken control of 1600 Pennsylvania Avenue, a generational shift not seen since JFK, with a broad mandate for change.

Meaning, of course, that cats have replaced dogs in the White House.

'Bye-bye, Millie. Cats, like baby boomers, have been steadily gaining power in this country since the early 1980s. And now the first boomer president brings the quintessential boomer pet to the White House: Socks the Cat.

This is an important issue that concerns all Americans, especially the fifty-seven million who own cats, the most popular companion animal in the nation, and who have been waiting since the disappointing Misty Mallarkey Ying Yang (Amy Carter's low-profile, non-photo-op feline) to get their claws back on the White House.

Ever since Abe Lincoln kept the first First Cat, felines have been an astonishingly rare White House breed, outnumbered by First Dogs (480!), First Birds (36), and even First Horses (11). Socks is only the tenth presidential cat.

You'd have to go back to the Coolidge administration, when Silent Cal went on the radio to ask folks to help look for Tiger, who'd run away, to find as big a moment in history for presidential kitties.

"This is a great day for cats," gushed Rachel Lamb, director of companion animals for the Humane Society of the United States in Washington, D.C. "Cats have had a tough history—burned at the stake and all that—and it's wonderful that a cat is now fit for the White House."

The day after Clinton's victory, Lamb huddled with White House officials to raise the questions on every American's mind: "Is Socks an indoor-outdoor cat? Is Socks declawed?"

And the most important question of all: *Does your cat in any way resemble John Bobbit?* (Yes/No)

Yes!

"We were whooping in the halls when we found out Socks was neutered," Lamb said. "We were screaming, 'Socks is neutered! Socks is neutered!' "

Lamb, like many animal lovers, was "very disappointed that the Bushes allowed Millie to breed, right down the street from the Washington shelter where thousands of animals are killed every day. It showed shocking ignorance and insensitivity to the pet overpopulation problem."

Yes, it looks like a proanimal administration. Al Gore is a famous supporter of endangered species, and his Labrador retriever and poodle are a heartbeat away from being First Pets. And the president endures weekly allergy shots, partly so Chelsea can keep her cat. Look for Chelsea to emerge as a national spokesperson for spay/neutering. And look for a run on homespun black-and-white cats from the pound. Adopting pets will be in; purebreds like Millie out. Another certainty: Of Clinton's first one hundred days, Socks will sleep right through sixty-seven. It will be the Year of the Cat.

Which brings us to the question: How did dogs, the most formidable of incumbents, get the boot? When Zeke, the family dog, died in 1990, Bill Clinton, like a lot of guys, wanted a dog. But, being a sensitive sort, he gave in to the two strong women in his life, who wanted a cat. Enter Socks, a gift from one of Chelsea's friends.

A true reformer would have made a bolder choice, harkening back to the days when Teddy Roosevelt kept a badger, and John Quincy Adams amused himself with silkworms.

"I think the American public is ready to see something new, be it a parrot or a boa constrictor," said presidential pet expert Niall Kelly. "It certainly would take the focus off the economy."

Still, Clinton should get a dog—a mutt—if only for populist photo opportunities, says Kelly, author of *Presidential Pets*. Kelly says only two presidents have had cats since 1932, Jimmy Carter and Gerald Ford, "and that's not an encouraging sign."

The First Siamese

Rutherford B. Hayes and his teetotaling First Lady, "Lemonade Lucy," like many austere people, seemed to prefer animals—including their pet canaries, goats, mockingbird, and greyhound—to people. Unfortunately their greyhound once stood directly in the way of the engine of American capitalism—i.e., a train. Whereupon David Sickels, U.S. ambassador to Siam, mailed the First Lady a Siamese cat, according to *Presidential Pets*.

"Dear Madam," he wrote, "I am taking the liberty of forwarding to you one of the finest specimens of Siamese cats that I have been able to procure in this country. Miss Pussy goes to Hong Kong whence she will be transhipped by the Occidental & Oriental Line . . . to San Francisco and then sent by express to Washington. I am informed that this is the first attempt ever made to send a Siamese cat to America."

On October 1, 1879, less than a year after "Lemonade Lucy" changed Miss Pussy's name to Siam, the cat died from illness.

Give That Cat Hell, Harry

Harry Truman was as disdainful of pets as he was of political opponents, never allowing an animal to become part of the family, according to *Presidential Pets*. When Mike the Magicat tried to find a home for himself by wandering onto the White House lawn, he was shipped home.

President Master at Moving a Cat

It's time for a "Wild Things" special report on presidential politics: President Clinton stumbled in his first one hundred days with his clumsy handling of the gays-in-the-military issue and his inability to hire an attorney general who did not employ a Dangerous Foreign and Illegal Baby-sitter, but everyone on the hill agreed—the new president aced his toughest challenge, which was, of course, moving Socks to the White House.

This should come as no surprise to anyone. Clinton vowed in his campaign that he'd have a peerless grasp of domestic issues. The new leader of the Western world set the tone for his administration on the morning after his stirring inaugural speech when he said to a woman in a red dress who was visiting the White House, "I really like your cat pin."

Whereupon, let history record, the chief executive of the United States presided over the absolutely textbook, effortless transition of Socks, the First Feline, to 1600 Pennsylvania Avenue, thereby giving the entire nation a primer on How to Properly Move a Cat.

This being a matter of urgent concern to cat owners, we called the Society Hill Veterinary Hospital in Philadelphia. "Oh goodness," said a technician, "you want to move a *cat*? I'd better get a doctor." Whereupon Dr. Virginia Lingle informed us that cats *hate* to move. Hate to move off a bed, hate to give up their favorite chair.

"So the best thing to do is to wait a month until you're settled into your new house before you move your cat. Wait until you've unpacked all your boxes, when you're not keeping the door open all day and the cat sneaks out.

We lost a lot of cats this way. Just wait until you're ready to be *totally focused on the cat."*

This, so far as we can determine, is exactly what happened at the White House.

After consulting with Little Rock veterinarian Dr. Joan Nafe, the First Family kept Socks back in Arkansas for three weeks, then the first First Cat in thirteen years arrived at the White House, driven across the country in Hillary's late-model Olds (flying is very stressful for cats), and was immediately locked with his litter box in the basement of the engineer's office.

This was also very good form. Cat shrink Mardie MacDonald devotes whole pages on the subject, "Moving Blues: The Value of the Special Room," in her book *The Cat Psychologist.* Cats are highly stressed in new surroundings (everyone who prizes their Oriental rugs knows what *highly stressed* cats are prone to do), and a special room helps them adjust.

Next, we called Rachel Lamb at the Humane Society, who had been busy since the inaugural trying to plumb secret sources in Arkansas to learn what Socks does all day.

Turns out that Socks, after spending days in the basement or the usher's room, slept in Chelsea's bed at night during this stressful transition.

Socks was also spotted purring happily on Chelsea's lap while the Clintons watched the Super Bowl, and being walked, on a leash, with a red harness and apparent tag, by two apparent Secret Service agents. (A collar and tag and leash are all good ideas for a newly moved cat, if your feline will take to the leash.)

After a cat gets over its new-house jitters, it begins to move happily from room to room, using its chin to apply a glandular oily secretion to sofas, chairs, and drapes, marking the entire house and everyone in it as its territory. A female cat will claim the front and back yards, and a male cat, like Socks, will stake out five acres, the Oval Office, and the National Security Council, and eventually remind everyone of Al Haig, who once said, "I'm in charge here!" This means the move has gone smoothly and everything is back to normal.

That'll Teach Him

Ida McKinley, beloved bride of President William McKinley, was so tickled when her Angora had four kittens, she named the two weaklings of the litter Valeriano Weyler, after the governor of Cuba, and Enrique DeLome, after the Spanish ambassador in Washington. Ha! Ha! The president loved this, until the Spanish-American War began to go badly for our side. Whereupon the First Lady ordered her maid to drown Valeriano Weyler and Enrique DeLome (the kittens). William McKinley was later assassinated.

Lonely Socks: Suicide Attempt?

Yes, spring 1993 was horrible for President Clinton, what with Waco, not to mention Bosnia. Then Socks, the famous First Cat, was found swinging by his leash from a tree on the White House lawn, nearly strangled to death.

A White House staffer saved Socks just in time, and an investigation revealed that Socks had not acted out of despair over the Senate jobs-bill defeat. He had simply climbed the tree, apparently tried to get down, and ended up swinging by the neck on part of his fifty-foot leash.

This was an unfortunate way for the president to mark Be Kind to Animals/National Pet Week (first week of May each year) and should remind all pet owners of that cat-behavior chestnut: "Don't let your cat hang itself from a tree."

It was especially troubling to Rachel Lamb of the Humane Society, which is conducting a worldwide Socks Look-Alike Contest. "What if Socks had died?" Lamb shuddered.

"We thought the Secret Service was walking Socks on his leash," Lamb added. "Apparently someone got lazy and said, 'I'm tired of watching Socks.' We recommend that cats never be let outside unsupervised." The Humane Society is still hoping someone from the White House—Chelsea, perhaps—will join Rue McClanahan of "The Golden Girls" to judge the contest.

Thousands of entries have poured in to try to win first prize, which includes a giant White House–replica cat bed. But no more entries will be accepted because men are starting to send pictures of themselves naked with black-and-white cats. Cats climb trees to get away from such owners.

Cats also climb to the uppermost branches to sleep and eat (in the case of some big cats, like jaguars) simply because they love to climb and because, Lam says, "In a tree they feel secure, less vulnerable in a new environment they're not quite adjusted to." We can see the headline if things don't straighten out at 1600 Pennsylvania Avenue: PRESIDENT REFUSES TO COME DOWN.

Post-Watergate Cats

Attempting to restore faith in government after Watergate, Gerald Ford brought a Siamese cat, Chan, to the White House. Chan, of course, was instantly forgotten by the nation once Liberty, the golden retriever, arrived and appeared in every presidential photograph from then on.

Democratic Fat Cat

Socks's movements through the White House are often monitored by a phalanx of serious, dark-suited men with wires on their ears. When the Humane Society delegation brought Lucy, the Socks Look-Alike Contest winner, to the White House to meet the actual First Cat, Socks appeared on leash and harness. "We were in an anteroom waiting for the presentation of Socks," Rachel Lamb said, "when we heard a burst of static and an apparent Secret Service agent say, 'The cat is now entering the West Wing.'"

JFK and Other Tomcats

John F. Kennedy imported a virtual ark to live at the White House, including numerous dogs, rabbits, lambs, ponies, guinea pigs, hamsters, horses, and deer—but only one short-staying cat, Tom Kitten. JFK was allergic to Tom Kitten, who was promptly exiled to live with the First Lady's secretary, Mary Gallagher.

Cabinet Scratching Post

Animal lovers who voted for President Clinton hardly en-
visioned the day Socks would be locked in the basement
and the president would be carrying a rifle around shooting at living things. If you're alarmed that the president
went duck shooting, Fund for Animals in New York City is
leading a letter-blitz on the White House (the White House
zip code is 20500; if you don't know the address by heart,
please immediately turn your pets over to a better family).

Meanwhile, Socks, the First Cat, was banished to the
White House basement because he can't keep his claws off
the new furniture, according to *Washingtonian* magazine.

We interrupt this report for a White House nondenial denial:
Deputy press secretary Neel Lattimore denies this, saying
only the State Dining Room is off-limits to Socks. An aide
to Hillary Rodham Clinton insisted Socks had "probably"
never seen the basement, but said he had been temporarily
banned from the State Dining Room, where the cat been
caught eyeing the seventy-five-pound gingerbread house.
"Socks had been nibbling on the little Socks-shaped gingerbread cookies hanging from the gingerbread house," a
source high in the administration told "Wild Things."

"Wild Things" is concerned that the First Family, and
many other families besides, don't know how to handle a
sofa-scratching cat. Here, then, are some Humane Society
tips: Buy a hemp or rope scratching post (cats prefer them
to the carpeted towers), place your cat's claws on the rope,
and shower him with catnip and praise. Tie inflated balloons to furniture under attack. Popped balloons, squirted
water, and other condemnations will keep kitty away.
Don't declaw your cat. "It's a form of mutilation," said a

Humane Society spokesman. "The top digit of the cat's finger is removed along with the claw."

A few weeks later, Socks had his revenge. Tourists in the State Dining Room were startled by the appearance of . . . a First Mouse! A little girl shrieked, and the mouse ran straight for the gingerbread house and began to nibble on Socks.

Kitty Hide-and-Seek

Calvin Coolidge used to lock his cat, Bounder, in bureau drawers, cupboards, and grandfather clocks so he and the First Lady could play "Guess which clockie-clockie kitty-kitty is hiding in." Then it was time for First Lady Grace to open her eyes and try to rescue the cats by listening for their meows. And critics say the Coolidges had no personality.

CHAPTER 3

YOUR HOUSE
CAT THINGS

IN WHICH WE REVEAL THE WORLD'S FATTEST CATS, AND
EXPLAIN HOW CATS RUIN HUMAN LOVE RELATIONSHIPS
AND KILL RUTHLESSLY IN FACT AND FICTION

**If Domestic Cats Are Truly Five Hundred Bengal Tigers in
Miniature, Why Don't They Eat Us While We Sleep?**

This question occurred to the "Wild Things" staff the day
we met the serial killer our wife-to-be affectionately called
"Boonie." Boonie was a sweet and loving black-and-white
cat who reminded us every autumn of the simple truths of
nature. He ate bluejays whole and left beheaded squirrels
in the backyard. Victoria Voith, who teaches animal behavior at the University of Florida, refuses to believe a
domestic cat this predatory existed. Alas, Boonie always
destroyed the evidence.

The day I met Boonie, he cornered me, the new boyfriend, in the living room. I felt, absurdly, like prey on

"Wild Kingdom." My palms beaded in sweat. I was wearing shorts! Don't laugh. It is indeed possible for a large adult cat, at least fifteen pounds with all its teeth and claws, to kill a human being. "But the cat would have to be behaving like a total maniac," says Philadelphia veterinarian Susan McDonough.

Suddenly, Boonie lunged. My leg spurted blood.

As I stepped over him to get a tissue, I wondered, Why did he stop there? After all, as that oft-rerun *National Geographic* special "Caressing the Tiger" reminds us, domestic cats mimic their big cousins in every way, including hunting.

What luck! We're just too big to bring down. "No predator is going to try to take down an animal that's ten to twenty times larger than it," said Voith. "It's just not efficient. Size is a major deterrent."

Another reason: They *love* us. Cats think we're their parents or we're their kittens. By breeding our cats for color and beauty, we've made the average kitty too nice to bite the hand that feeds it.

For the record, there's no known case of a domestic cat killing a person. Sure, bites and scratches, a hospitalization here and there . . . but the people almost always deserved it.

How Can I Stop a Cat from Ruining My Sex Life?

Cats can be hazardous to the health of marriages and other human relationships. Jealous cats have been known to bite boyfriends, kill kittens, and defecate all over the house when an owner gets married. They can even go into Major Rejection Funks and vomit, develop ulcers, and refuse to eat.

"They get right in the middle, spoon their back against you, and push the boyfriend away," says McDonough. Cats hate it when you cat around.

McDonough once received a frantic late-night call from a woman who was having an affair with a married man. The cat showed his displeasure by urinating in the man's shoes. McDonough's advice: "Stop seeing married men."

Whether such behavior indicates a cat is behaving like a jealous teenager or a temperamental toddler isn't clear. Science is still pondering this question. "We don't know if a cat can actually be jealous because we can't talk to the animal," says Dr. Katherine Houpt, director of the Animal Behavior Clinic at Cornell University. "I'm not sure whether cats have the mental ability to be jealous. Presumably their brain development is that of an eighteen-month-old child. We know they get stressed over a new boyfriend or a new baby and do things like urinate outside the litter box."

Here's what to do with lovelorn felines: Neuter a mature cat to calm him down. Let the married man or other aggrieved mate feed kitty to forge a bond. Smother the cat with love. "When you have a second child and the first child is acting out," McDonough says, "you give the first child more attention than he really wants and he goes away."

Cat psychologist Peter Neville advised one beleaguered husband to get down on the floor on all fours and "mimic feline greeting behaviors." After weeks of this, the wife reported her husband was "a totally reformed character who had given up all signs of macho, short-tempered, and dominating behavior in the home for fear of upsetting the cat."

How Do Cats Suffocate Babies?

This is an old wives' tale. We asked Dr. Karen Overall of the University of Pennsylvania's animal behavior clinic, who said: "You mean, Do black cats crawl into babies' cribs and suck the breath out of their mouths? Ha. Ha. Ha. Hold on, let me ask my students. [*Cupping phone. Unrestrained laughter in the behavior clinic.*] No. Of course not."

It's hard to believe the myth of baby-killing cats is still with us from the Dark Ages, when those evil witches' accomplices were virtually eliminated from Europe. "I think most of these deaths can be attributed to infant-death syndrome," says behaviorist Voith, "and there just happened to be a cat in the house."

Overall says she knows of two infant deaths in recent years where a dog or cat apparently got in the crib and snuggled too close. "It's unclear whether it was the animal's body or the blanket doing the suffocating."

This unlikely tragedy is easily averted. Use a baby monitor. Shut the baby's door at night until the infant is six to eight months old and can sit up and take care of itself. After that, beware: Pets kill babies with kindness.

Why Do Cats Get Chummy with the One Person in the Room Who Hates Cats?

Cats *hate* to be stared at. In feline terms, a stare is mildly threatening behavior. So when a cat walks into a room, the people who are gawking and waving are frightening the cat. These, of course, are the *cat lovers*. The cat gratefully approaches the one person who's *not* staring at him, who is in fact staring away and silently praying the cat will disappear. This is the *cat hater*. To the hater's horror, the appreciative feline begins to rub his leg and jumps on his lap. If you're cat-phobic and would rather avoid this, Desmond Morris advises, "Lean toward a cat, stare fixedly at it with wide-open eyes, and make agitated hand movements," begging the cat to sit on your lap. If you do this emphatically for ten minutes, we personally guarantee the cat will look for another lap. And the hostess will look for another friend.

How Do Cats Survive Thirty-Story Falls?

I have some very good news for those of you who have committed the unforgivable lapse of not paying attention to your cat at all times and thereby allowing Morris to leap thirty stories out an open window: He will land on his stomach and not be hurt.

Scientists in New York City have proven this remarkable phenomenon in a study of 132 cats that fell an average of 5.5 stories out of tall buildings: Ninety percent of them survived, including Sabrina, who fell thirty-two stories and chipped a tooth, and was hungry because she'd traveled a long way without eating.

Special note: Dr. Wayne Whitney and Dr. Cheryl Mehlaff of the Animal Medical Center in Manhattan have had their lives ruined by reporting this research and want to emphasize that *they did not throw 132 cats out of skyscraper windows on purpose*. The cats just fell. Since High-Rise Syndrome, or HRS, has been reported from Los Angeles to Miami to Washington, D.C., during the past few summers, "Wild

Things" would like to offer a safety guide to Frequent Flier Felines:

Move to a higher floor. Among thirteen felines that fell more than nine floors, there was only one fracture and no deaths. This is because after falling about five stories cats spread their arms like wings, imitating squirrels, scientists suppose, parachuting to the ground on their bellies and softening the impact. Cats are believed to have nine lives because of their remarkable ability to land on their feet, but HRS superstars survive by landing stomach-first. In shorter falls, cats do land on their feet, causing greater injury (fractures and hemorrhages are common) but few deaths.

Don't try this at home. Cats, remarkably, study the horizon (even at night) and torque themselves right-side-up for a proper landing in the *first three feet of a fall*. Then they reach a maximum speed of 60 miles per hour while cruising in for a gentle landing. Humans, however, tumble out of skyscraper windows at disastrous angles and reach an impressive maximum speed of 120 miles per hour. People cannot be taught to right themselves like cats, experts say. It's innate.

Don't assume cat intelligence. If cats are so graceful and smart, why do they fall out open windows? Sixty-four percent of "high-fliers" are two and a half years old or younger and are making the bad judgments of young creatures everywhere. Cats, so confident of their superior balance, commonly play on open ledges, leap for insects, or tumble in playful kitty duos out the window. In Dade County, Florida, where a Himalayan named Bailey is the HRS record-holder, with a twenty-four-story injury-free flight, cats leap after taunting birds. "The cat leaps at the bird. The bird flies away. The cat keeps going," says a Miami vet. "Cats are instinctive hunters." Alas, cats can't judge depth. Ten stories look like two stories to them.

Don't let your dogs try this. Dogs are more careful around the window ledge, but in eighty-one cases in New York over several years, canines chased a squirrel, cat, other dog, and, in one case, a burglar, right out the window. Dogs also reach impressive speeds in midair and don't fare as well as cats landing on sidewalks from great distances.

Don't assume human intelligence. Falling pets are common in summertime, when it gets so hot people just fling open the ol' window. We recommend a window air conditioner, and Dr. Whitney suggests investing in a remarkable light-weight perforated aluminum technology that allows air to pass in and keeps cats and dogs from going out. "Put in a window screen."

How Do Cats Kill Their Prey?

The aptly named "killing bite." Yes, your ordinary house and yard cat and the jungle Bengal tiger use the same, time-honored technique. Once the cat, big or small, domestic or wild, seizes its prey, it swiftly bites the back of the neck, using long "canine" teeth to sever the spinal cord. Some researchers believe cats find just the right place to bite the neck by the lie of the hairs on a mouse or feathers on a bird. To accomplish the complete bite that must pass between the vertebrae to break the spinal chord, cats must "feel" with their canine teeth, according to veterinarian Michael Fox. The base of canine teeth is loaded with special nerve receptors just for this "feeling" purpose, which proves cats have feelings too.

Where Does Kitty Litter Come From?

Kitty litter deposits are extracted from the earth in vast open-pit mining operations overseen by the fat cats of the industry, litter-box barons whose ears burn every time someone calls them "Kitty Litter Kings." In fact millions of cats dig around in piles of Fresh Step and countless other brands every day, and still their manufacturers can't escape the long shadow of Kitty Litter!

Time for a trademark lesson: The proper generic term is kitty litter—note the lowercase *kl*—or cat litter. Kitty Litter is the trademarked name for a brand of granulated clay cat-box filler so dominant that we mistake it for the generic. And for this we have to blame the legendary American mogul Ed Lowe—"the Kitty Litter King of Cassopolis"—Cassopolis being the small town in south-central Michigan where in 1947 a bunch of farmers crossed the sensible ecological divide that had separated the species for nine millennia and permanently invited cats inside to poop.

How this happened is a rural myth as quaint as "How Superman Came to Earth." Lowe was working in his father's sawdust business, which sold absorbent clay to soak up oil and grease. One day a friend, Kay Draper, asked him for some sand for her cat box. Instead, Lowe gave her a bag of the clay, and it worked so well Lowe was soon peddling the stuff from the trunk of his '43 Chevy. Whereupon something remarkable happened in the history of capitalism prior to the current Soviet model: No one else bothered to market kitty litter for ten years!

By 1990 the grand old patriarch of cat poop had built the entire $600 million kitty litter industry, a nationwide company with five strip-mining operations, and a vast personal fortune (including mansions around the world, private planes, his own railroad) on an incalculably large pile of feline doo-doo. Actually it *can* be roughly calculated: Cat owners in the United States buy enough kitty litter each year to fill the Empire State Building two and a half times. *Whew!*

Why did this happen, when for years folks got by with shredded newspaper, crushed corn husks, and oat flakes?

Simply put, cat litter works better. We weren't sure exactly why, so we called the kitty litter lobby, which, of course, has an office in Washington, D.C., so it can keep an eye on Congress. It calls itself the Sorptive Minerals Institute, which is very impressive on a letterhead, and a name Congress members cannot take lightly. Most commercial cat litters are made from fuller's earth, it turns out, an inelastic brown clay that is one of the most absorbent substances on the planet. "It's amazing," asserts Steve Hellem, executive director of the Sorptive Minerals Institute. "It absorbs anywhere from 50 to 70 percent of its weight in moisture and holds it very well."

The largest known deposits of fuller's earth lie in Florida, Georgia, the Midwest, and California, where the litter giants tear away five-foot "overburdens" to find deposits, crush cat-litter boulders into pebbles, and add highly secretive blends of chemical deodorants. Now seventy, Lowe often says, "If I hadn't run into Kay that day, I'd still be shoveling sawdust." And approximately 29 percent of American homes (especially the 5 percent that keep the box in the bedroom) would smell a heck of a lot worse.

What States Have the Most Cats?

After a lengthy investigation, "Wild Things" has learned the true reason behind the Sun Belt migration. California has the most cats! (The Rust Belt has the fewest.) Overall, the Pacific region boasts the highest population of pet cats, according to a survey by the American Veterinary Association. California, Oregon, and Washington have a feline population of 5.2 million (picture a city bigger than Detroit, all cats). The mid-Atlantic region (New York, New Jersey, and Pennsylvania) have the fewest cats, with 3.8 million (27 percent of households), which explains, we think, why people are leaving the Rust Belt.

What's the Best Way to Introduce a Cat and a Baby?

After a careful counting of strollers in our town, the "Wild Things" staff has determined that June is baby month, when proud parents bring the newborn home from the hospital to meet the creature who, until this fateful moment, has been *the focus of love and center of the entire universe*.

This is, of course, the cat. Cats cause havoc in the house of new birth. They want to sleep in the crib. They want a pet from Mommy. They want to breast-feed, too. And who can blame them? The mother-in-law, who runs around providing invaluable help and also repeating ancient superstitions such as "You have a baby, now you have to get rid of the cat." (Which *their* mothers-in-law told them and so on, all the way back to the Middle Ages.) Too many new moms heed this advice, and for them we have a Guide to Safely Introducing Baby and Kitty.

Keep the cat and relax. Susan McDonough, who owns the Cat Hospital in Philadelphia, has never heard of a cat (who wasn't already bad-tempered) attacking a newborn child as an enemy. (If this extreme rarity happens, shoot the cat with a water pistol. It will get the message.) The medieval myth of cats sucking out the breath of a sleeping baby is also just that, an unfounded myth. McDonough let March, her baby daughter, sleep in a cat carrier in the Cat Hospital. And Joe, her cat, slept beside the baby. So? "I didn't worry," McDonough says. "Of course, I also didn't worry when my baby was spitting up furballs, which she had gotten by crawling around the floor of the Cat Hospital. Might I suggest the headline VET'S BABY SPITS UP CAT FURBALLS?" You don't have to be *this* casual, but a casual attitude is instructive. Relax.

Include kitty. What does a cat typically get for his great interest in the new family? Shoo, shoo. Slam, slam. The cat's revenge is not to attack but to indulge in what vets call "house urea," which sounds like one of the royal families on the planet Dune but is actually "a popular euphemism for your cat urinating and defecating all over the house in response to a new baby," McDonough says. The classic analogy is Dr. Spock: "Your two-year-old child is toilet-trained until the baby comes home, then your two-year-old is not toilet-trained anymore. It's an unconscious anxiety response, and the solution is the same." Make an effort to make the kitty feel like part of the family by, say, letting him sit on a nearby chair during breast-feeding.

Let the cat sniff Baby. Karen Overall of the University of Pennsylvania's veterinary school's behavior clinic recommends letting the cat sniff the newborn's clothes before the baby comes home. It will make the cat comfortable with the new scent in the house. Overall suggests building in at least five minutes' daily quality time with the displaced cat (a pat on the head is a well-spent second). Keep that cat out of the baby's room if you wish (shutting the door at night is a good idea). At five months, you'll be stopping the baby from pulling poor kitty's tail. At seven years, March's age now, she'll try to ride the dog. But that's another column.

Can I Depreciate My Cat?

People will try anything! One dog owner tried to pass off thousands of dollars in vet bills as his own deductible medical expenses, Philadelphia accountant David Lidle told "Wild Things." This actually worked until the auditor noticed the "D.V.M."—doctor of veterinary medicine—on the bills. A racetrack owner was able to depreciate his greyhounds. But generally the answer is no. "You can't claim a dog or cat or any pet as a personal exemption. You can't depreciate them," says IRS spokesman Henry Holmes in Washington. "But if it's a business—such as breeding animals—you can report the income and deduct the expenses." Owners of show dogs and cats spend as much as $100,000 a year keeping their pets on the road, but no income is generated. It's just for prestige, which cannot be deducted.

What Is the World's Fattest Cat?

This being 1993, the Year of the Cat, "Wild Things" was investigating several serious and important feline issues such as *What is the world's fattest cat?* and *Diet tips for overweight cats*, when we saw this headline in one of our nation's newspapers: WORLD'S BIGGEST CAT TIPS SCALE AT 78 POUNDS! KING KONG KITTY WEIGHS AS MUCH AS AN 11-YEAR-OLD BOY! HE EATS 90 CANS OF TUNA A WEEK!

Now the "Wild Things" household has a special interest in large cats, since we are awakened three nights a week by the terrifying *thud-thud-thud* of a strange intruder on the stairs, only to realize it is Buddy, our eighteen-pounder, buffaloing his way to the kitchen for a snack. So naturally we had to investigate this report in the *Weekly World News*, which, of course, is the newspaper of record for animal stories no one else has—such as, in the April 6, 1993 issue alone, SPACE ALIENS KILLING ALABAMA CATTLE! and GOOFY GOOSE FALLS IN LOVE—WITH A TRAFFIC CONE! Okay, so we couldn't find conclusive evidence that Fluffy, the seventy-eight-pounder, of Danville, Connecticut, where Fluffy lives, or Marybelle Bresk, his thirty-one-year-old divorcée owner, who is pictured getting a hernia as she lifts and hugs Fluffy, actually exist. (Marybelle, please contact us immediately if you exist!) But we did learn:

Himmy was the heaviest! The fattest cat for which reasonably sound documentation exists was Himmy (short, we think, for Himalayan), of Red Lynch, Queensland, Australia, according to *The Guinness Book of World Records*. At the time of his death on March 12, 1986, from respiratory failure, Himmy, age ten, weighed forty-six pounds fifteen and one-quarter ounces, and, judging by his thirty-three-inch waist and thirty-eight-inch overall length, was almost perfectly square. Unconfirmed, *Guinness* reports, is the existence of one Mr. Edward Bear of Sydney, New South Wales, Australia, a forty-eight-pound feline.

Tiddles may exist! Before Fluffy, the *Weekly World News* reported that Tiddles, a fifty-one-pounder owned by Miss June Watson of London, England, was the world's fattest cat. The *Philadelphia Inquirer* reported this story too, and fifty-one pounds is a possible weight for a cat, according to Susan McDonough, who does not believe that seventy-eight pounds is felinely feasible. In the following month's collector's edition, the *Weekly World News* reported that Tiddles eats five pork chops, a pound of cheese, two pounds of fish, and three quarts of fresh sweet cream *daily*. And Hitler was a woman.

8.6 pounds is average. Yes, the average adult male cat weighs a mere 8.6 pounds, the average adult female 7.2 pounds, according to *Guinness*. You can increase these weights a pound or two for pampered pets, McDonough says. But if your cat tips the scales into the teens and is *not* a Maine coon, which runs fifteen to twenty pounds, or, like Buddy, a Maine coon–Sears Coldspot mix, watch this space for future fat-cat diet tips.

Why Are Cats, the Nation's Most Popular Pet, Portrayed as Ruthless Killers in Crime Novels?

This is one of the strangest pet trends of the nineties. As our most popular pets are celebrated in the Year of the Cat, cats are portrayed as serial killers and hard-hearted detectives in a new subgenre of the crime novel: the cat mystery. "There's a huge boom in cat crime novels," says Ed

Gorman, publisher of *Mystery Scene* magazine and editor of three "Cat Crimes" mystery anthologies. "Cats have been associated with mystery novels since Poe wrote 'The Black Cat,' but never like this," Gorman says. John D. McDonald dedicated *The End of Night* to his cat Roger, "who left his tracks on the manuscript." Raymond Chandler adored his cat Taki and once wrote: "By gad, sir . . . if you hate [cats], I may learn to hate you. . . . We have a black Persian cat nearly nineteen years old which we would not exchange for one of the topless towers of Manhattan." For new beach-blanket thrills, "Wild Things" suggests:

Rita Mae Brown. The respected author of *Rubyfruit Jungle* has written two cat mysteries, including *Rest in Pieces* (Bantam), which features a cat, a Welsh corgi, and other critters.

Carole Nelson Douglas. Douglas's witty thrillers are partly narrated by a smart-aleck cat, Midnight Louie. In her latest, *Pussyfoot*, Vegas PR flack Temple Barr and ex-hotel cat Midnight Louie track down Jack the Stripper-ripper on the Strip.

Felidae. Dark and literary, compared to *Perfume* and *The Name of the Rose*, is Turkish-born novelist Akif Pirincci's *Felidae*. Detective Francis, a house cat, pursues a serial decapitator of cats and sets into motion a hideous social experiment.

Lilian Jackson Braun. The Queen of Cat Writers' fifteenth book, *The Cat Who Went into the Closet*, quickly became a best-seller. Newspaper columnist Jim Qwilleran solves another murder with the help of his cats, Koko and Yum Yum. "Cats are mysterious, perverse, independent and funny," Braun says. "And they are so beautiful and charming, they can get away with murder."

How Do Cats Predict Earthquakes?

Cats' astonishing foreknowledge about disasters and ordinary events, such as an owner's return home, can be explained by rational minds. Too bad. The best stories are inexplicable to science.

With their powerful sense of hearing and smell, cats can detect a slight tremor heralding an earthquake and a faint smell signaling a fire long before we can, giving owners the misimpression that their cat is clairvoyant, according to veterinarian Michael Fox.

Similarly, a cat uses its authentic sensory powers—senses that are far keener than ours—to predict your arrival home from work each day and be waiting for you on the stoop. Anyone awakened by the cold nose of a cat at the same time every morning knows the exquisite time clock in a cat's head. Cats have a remarkable sense of timing that is crucial in nature to be a predator, avoid predators, and survive in the wild.

If you prefer the theories on Cat ESP—there are more books on Cat ESP than books on U.S. presidents—go right ahead. But Desmond Morris scoffs at that malarkey. "ESP enthusiasts . . . prefer the cat to remain a mystic feline force among us," he says.

Fat Cat Diet Tips

Despite what you read in *The Economist*, there's compelling new evidence in the *Journal of the American Veterinary Medical Association* that America is still a great civilization with vast resources and leisure time. Our pets are setting records for doing nothing and growing hideously fat! Alas, dog and cat obesity is a disturbing national problem that saps our global competitiveness, since fat cats and double-chinned Chihuahuas are created by *lazy and undisciplined American workers*. Yes, a new study shows that 44 percent of all companion animals in America are overweight, *JAVMA* says, and "the weight treatment program must be directed toward the owner's behavior, rather than the pet's." The *JAVMA* pet diet program is based on principles of classic and operant conditioning developed by Ivan Pavlov and B. F. Skinner, and successfully applied to human obesity, as follows:

Life is not a carnival cruise. Some pet owners foolishly feed their animals four times a day with a midnight pasta buffet. Most pets should be fed once or twice daily. If Spot must have snacks, reduce mealtime consumption, says *JAVMA* author and veterinarian Bonnie Beaver.

Stimulus-control modification. This is the scientific way of saying, Do not slide pineapple-glazed chicken breasts under the table. Hard for some to believe, *JAVMA* says, but "the animal should be given food only in his bowl," on a rigid schedule followed by all family members. This limits the cues associated with eating and minimizes begging.

Give them something to do. It's a matter of national pride that our pets have nothing to do but angle for pleasure, but dogs are happier and thinner if they have regular important tasks, like chasing saliva-covered tennis balls. Yes, cats normally sleep twenty hours a day, but you must rouse them to play. There have been few improvements on a toy at the end of a string.

Cats can't crash-diet. Careful: Cats are so finicky they will go on the well-known Bobby Sands Feline Fast if they don't like their diet food. Cats get obsessed with shape.

(Recently recorded cat quote in southern New Jersey: "Yuck, stars! Stars! Where are the salmon hexagons?! Who trained these people!? I'd rather die!") Dogs and people can cut way down without (immediate) harmful health effects, but cats can't metabolize all the broken-down fat of a crash diet, says Laurie Sponza of the University of Pennsylvania's veterinary school. It can cause hepatic lipidosis, a potentially fatal fatty liver condition.

CHAPTER 4

WHITE HOUSE
DOG THINGS

IN WHICH TWO CENTURIES OF PRESIDENTS KILL
AND ABUSE THEIR FIRST DOGS—USING MURDER,
A TRAIN, POISON, A CAR, EXILE, AND DISGRACE;
BUSH BLOWS THE ELECTION BY MISHANDLING MILLIE;
AND CLINTON LEAVES A HOMELESS MUTT TO DIE

Shortly after his historic election, William Jefferson Clinton courted certain disaster by announcing to the American people the most revolutionary part of his domestic policy:

The president of the United States *would not have a dog.*

Yes, an important rule of American politics, aside from "Never say no to a special interest group," is that the president must have a dog. This rule was instituted by George Washington, who had thirty-four hunting dogs, including Drunkard, Tipsy, Sweetlips, and the sex-crazed Madame Moose. "A new coach dog has arrived for the benefit of Madame Moose," Washington once wrote in his diary. "Her amorous fits should therefore be attended to."

The Father of Our Country was a true animal lover, keeping many farm animals and a parrot, and distinguishing himself as the finest dog owner of all our presidents. He was, however, so disdainful of *actual people* that he wore white gloves so he wouldn't have to press the common flesh.

In this way Washington passed on an inspiring legacy that made this country great: the whole noble experiment in democracy, the dollar bill, and the hardy Anglo-Saxon principle Never Show Weakness to Actual People; Dogs Are Your Friends. At the end of his presidency, in a fit of nostalgia, Washington wrote, "On the one side I am called upon to remember the parrot, and on the other to remember the dog. For my own part I should not pine much if both were forgot." True, this is not how we define the term *dog lover* today, but America was a much different place then, in that the NBA only had three Atlantic Division teams and dunking was illegal. Washington was our first true dog lover simply because (a) he had thirty-four dogs, and (b) none of them died horribly.

The same could not be said of Madame Moose's successors. After examining the tragic history of First Dogs, "Wild Things" has documented 3,288 instances in which presidents focused on foreign policy and economic issues to divert public attention from the fact that *our First Dogs were being treated even worse than our First Cats.* To wit:

Lincoln's Dog Was Assassinated

Yes, Abraham Lincoln, whose birthday we celebrate on Lincoln's Birthday, had a loyal yellow dog named Fido, but Lincoln pawned Fido off on a friend when he left for the

White House, according to Niall Kelly in *Presidential Pets*. Lincoln went to save the Union; Fido went to live with John Eddy Roll in Springfield, Illinois. Lincoln was assassinated by John Wilkes Booth. Fido was stabbed to death by a drunken man in a psychotic rage.

Rutherford B. Hayes's Dog Was Killed by a Train

President Hayes, a famous animal lover, was given a lovely brindle greyhound called Grim by William DuPont. In the spring of 1885, Grim met an ending that lived up to his name. "The death of Grim has made us all mourn," the former president wrote in his diary of March 5, 1885, according to *Name That Dog*, by Lynne M. Hamer. "He was killed instantly by a train on the Lake Shore Railroad at Pease's Crossing. He stood on the track evidently expecting the train to turn out for him . . . his head was taken clear off—also his foreleg. His remains will be buried when the frost is out of the ground on Cemetery Point, by the side of 'Old Whitney' and 'Old Ned.' "

Ulysses S. Grant's Dogs Were Murdered in the White House

In the 1870s several dogs acquired by President Ulysses S. Grant for his son Jessie died mysteriously, apparently killed by White House staff, according to *Presidential Pets*. When Jesse got a Newfoundland pup named Faithful, the president summoned his entire staff and barked: "Jesse has a new dog. You may have noticed that his former pets have been peculiarly unfortunate. When this dog dies every employee in the White House will be at once discharged." Faithful lived a long, happy life.

William Henry Harrison Tried to Exploit His Dog for Political Gain

History reserves the lowest place for *presidents who tried to exploit dogs for political gain.* William Henry Harrison, who was raised in a Virginia mansion, used a phony log cabin as the central image of his campaign, complete with a campaign lithograph showing a phonied-up faithful dog happily greeting a one-legged soldier outside the log cabin. Harrison died of pneumonia a month into his first term.

Warren G. Harding Tried to Compromise His Dog's Integrity During the Teapot Dome Scandal

Warren G. Harding never missed a chance to divert attention from the Teapot Dome scandal by trumpeting the virtues of his fine Airedale, Laddie Boy, who even gave "interviews" to reporters. Harding died mysteriously in San Francisco and went disgraced into history as the worst president of all time. Laddie Boy is remembered by many as the finest member of the Harding administration.

LBJ Got Us Into Vietnam and Picked Up His Beagles by the Ears

In an April 1964 meeting with bankers, LBJ casually picked up his two beagles, Him and Her, by the ears, outraging thousands of Americans. The president's popularity ratings plummeted. Dog lovers called for the president to be neutered without anesthesia or at least explain why he did it. "To make them bark," LBJ growled. "It's good for them." In 1966 Him was struck and killed by a car while chasing a squirrel on the White House grounds. Her died on the operating table as veterinarians tried to remove a large rock she had swallowed.

Truman Admired LBJ for Picking Up His Beagles by the Ears

Ex-president "Give 'em hell, Harry," Truman came to LBJ's defense in the beagle scandal: "What the hell are the critics hollering about? That's the way to handle hounds."

Truman's Dog Suffers from Truman and Rickets

When Postmaster General Bob Hannegan gave Mike, the Irish setter, to the First Lady, the Trumans kept whining about the dog's overexuberance and dumped Mike off on a farm in Virginia. But not before feeding him so much candy the dog developed rickets.

Hoover Worked His Dog to Death

Herbert Hoover was so cold and humorless his advisers sent thousands of copies of a friendly shot of the candidate with his great German shepherd King Tut to voters. It worked, and the "dog lover" was elected. Alas, Hoover allowed King Tut to work himself to death. Tut died a frail, shrunken version of himself, from trying to guard every White House gate.

Eisenhower Banished His Dog for Peeing on the Rug

One Sunday morning when, we imagine, President Eisenhower was golfing, the First Lady frantically summoned Ike's chief of staff:

"Mr. West, can you come down right away, we have a terrible problem in the Diplomatic Room." The problem was a big yellow spot on the brand-new carpet, left by Heidi, the First Weimaraner. "The very next day," Niall Kelly reports, "the rug was sent out to be dyed and Heidi was sent to the Eisenhower farm in Gettysburg."

Both Roosevelts Exiled Their Dogs for Biting

Teddy Roosevelt liked to say, "I feel like a bull moose!" but he didn't feel like keeping his bull terrier. The dog nipped so many legs TR shipped him to Long Island. Franklin Delano Roosevelt's German shepherd, Major, took a chunk out of the leg of U.S. senator Hattie Caraway, ripped the trousers off British prime minister Ramsay MacDonald, and was exiled by FDR to the Roosevelt home in Hyde Park.

Nixon's Dog Left the White House in Disgrace

Poor King Timahoe, the noble Irish setter who belonged to Richard Nixon. Nixon named him Timahoe for the chief executive's ancestral Irish village and King because "If he's the presidential dog he will be treated like a king, won't he?" Nixon said. Outraged Americans, who thought they'd elected a president and not a king, forced Nixon to change the name to Timahoe.

Reagan Got Rid of Lucky for Pulling on His Leash

Petite Nancy Reagan just couldn't handle the big sheepdog Lucky. Quipped a White House staffer: "It looks like the First Lady is waterskiing behind the dog." Lucky was exiled to the Reagans' California ranch.

Why Did Populist Bill Clinton Try to Buy the Most Elitist, Overpriced Dog on Earth, the "Blond Bimbo" of Breeds?

Uh-oh. A new national poll reveals that 60 percent of Americans believe immigration to be bad. And the president of the United States has declared his intention to purchase a golden retriever puppy.

If these seem unconnected, remember this: So did Jack Kennedy and Marilyn Monroe, at first.

The fact is, Bill Clinton is on the brink of a major domestic faux paw with grave social implications. The populist Democrat, swept into office on the promise of prudent economics and compassion for all, is shopping for one of the most overpriced and elitist dogs on earth, an animal cynically inbred into such drooling brainless exuberance that it will cheerfully chase a thrown ball at full speed into a tree and bounce off as unhurt as if its head were made of latex, which in a way it is. Among breeders and veterinarians and dog experts worldwide, the golden is known as the bimbo of breeds.

Suffice it to say that Gerald Ford owned a golden, and people often commented that Liberty was very much like the president. They both had pleasantly square heads. None of this would be particularly noteworthy were it not for the fact that President Clinton is pursuing a golden with the same fervor as a golden pursuing a Frisbee off the deck of an aircraft carrier. In May 1993, the president bid $3,500 for a golden retriever at a charity auction at Sidwell Friends School, where daughter Chelsea is a student. Fortunately he was outbid.

Undaunted, the president then tried to purchase Chelsea a golden retriever puppy owned by Robert Wood Johnson IV, whose great-grandfather was a founder of Johnson & Johnson. Again, fortunately, Clinton was too late. Laurence and Mary Rockefeller had already picked a puppy, and the last two went to Revlon chairman Ronald O. Perelman, who whisked his pups away by helicopter. I wish I were making this up.

These events have alarmed animal lovers everywhere, including the president's late mother. The late Virginia Kelley, I am informed, once exclaimed to an official of the Humane Society, "Why, I bet that rascal never even thought of going to an animal shelter! I'll get on him!"

Bill, you rascal, listen to your mama. Or better yet, listen to your hero, John Kennedy, who once said something very nearly like this about his beloved America: "We are a nation of mutts." Kennedy's point, had he actually made it, was profound.

In his book *The Decline of the West*, German historian Oswald Spengler said all cultures go through a life cycle and that the United States had passed its maturity and was already heading into an imminent decline from which there was no escape. Spengler made this prediction in 1922. He was spectacularly wrong, of course, possibly because he did not consider the salubrious effects of America's robust immigration, a constant churning of a nation's genetic material that works against the ravages of social stagnation, and makes it forever young. Geneticists have a name for this phenomenon. They call it "hybrid vigor." It is a good thing.

Critics of immigration, the 60 percent of you, take note. We have always been a nation of mongrels. It is what makes us strong. Well, it is the same with dogs.

Perhaps the president is under the misimpression, like many Americans, that purebred dogs are actually superior to mutts. The truth is, most of our nation's purebreds are like the etiolated descendants of once-vigorous great families, feebly dignified aristocrats who can no longer afford the upkeep of the manor house.

The golden, as we've noted, has had the smarts bred right out of it, and it is subject to many genetic diseases that never trifle most hardy mutts.

Cocker spaniels? The president's previous dog, Zeke, was a cocker, who was hit by a car when the president was governor of Arkansas. Cockers not only have floppy ears that easily get infected, and have had most of the common sense and purpose bred right out of them, they are, in the words of one of the country's best dog trainers, Brian Kilcommons, "horrible little dogs" who climbed to the top of the biting charts as their popularity soared.

This is the purebred phenomenon, genetic sloppiness fed by greed. See, purebreds have cycles. Just like totalitarian, xenophobic societies. Read Spengler. But this is not true with mutts. "If you breed two inbred lines together," says noted dog geneticist Harris Dunlap, "you end up with superior traits."

It is important to note, then, that if the security of the West comes down to a sled-dog race between President Clinton's dogs and, say, Boris Yeltsin's team, well, we should of course be exporting our fine golden retrievers to Russia as gifts.

Meanwhile our wonderful mutts are being gassed. Millions of them are put to death each year. Rather than squandering $3,500 on a golden pup, Mr. President, why not adopt a shelter dog for about $35? It's a matter of decency, but also economics. The furious national euthanasia of these perfectly good pets costs taxpayers $3 to $5 per person per year. Not to mention the absurd cost of health care for beagles with glaucoma, Labs with bad hips, deaf Dalmatians, cockers with ear infections.

Prudent choices in holding down health care costs, Mr. President. If you don't believe me, ask the missus.

So. I'd like to recommend the Washington Humane Society on Georgia Avenue NW, fifteen minutes from the White House. It's a heartbreaking place, run by good people. Go there tomorrow. Take Chelsea. Pick an old dog. A fat dog. An ungainly dog. A dog with preposterous ears. A dog who is going to die tomorrow, if you don't take him. Humane Society spokesperson Rosemary Vozobule cautions that you will have to submit to a qualifying "home visit" just like everyone else, but she feels confident you will pass.

Give the nation a three-minute network-TV lesson on helping the disadvantaged and keeping down health costs. It'll be a half hour on CNN, the front page of the nation's newspapers, and you'll be honored for it always.

Do it for your daughter.

Do it for your mom.

Editor's note: The above story appeared on the front page of the *Washington Post* "Style" section of August 8, 1993, with a photograph of a five-month-old shepherd mix at the Washington Humane Society named Gemini. The caption urged the president to immediately adopt the mutt Gemini before the dog was gassed. Numerous callers contacted the *Post*, the White House, and the Humane Society inquiring about Gemini's fate.

The president never called. The White House never put in a single word about Gemini. After five weeks, "We were disappointed we never heard from the White House," says animal care manager Michelle Williams. But Gemini was adopted by Crystal Beslow, a Washington police officer and single mother with two children. "Wild Things" received many letters from readers who said they never would have voted for Clinton had they known his position on dogs.

Mutts versus Purebreds: LBJ Learned the Hard Way

LBJ adored Blanco (Spanish for "white"), his rare and totally neurotic pure-white collie. Alas, Blanco peed (Spanish for "yellow") all over an Alexander Calder sculpture on loan to the White House from the Museum of Modern Art. Then Blanco bit LBJ's dog Edgar, a gift from J. Edgar Hoover. In the end LBJ's favorite pooch was Yuki, a stray mongrel that Luci (the president's daughter) found at a Texas gas station. Yuki was an instantly recognizable breed, *the very small white dog*. The mutt sat in on cabinet meetings, watched legislation signed in the East Room, shook paws with the Joint Chiefs, and was the subject of a biography by Luci.

Calvin Coolidge Was Nice to Dogs

Silent Cal, like the Father of Our Country, was another president who had problems warming up to actual people but loved his dogs. Wrote Will Rogers after dining in the Coolidge White House: "They was feeding the dogs so much that . . . it looked like the dogs was getting more than me. . . . I come pretty near to getting on my all-fours and barking."

How Did George Bush's Mishandling of the "Millie Thing" Cost Him the White House?

Yes, George never grasped the "dog thing."

The most popular Republican in the United States during the Bush years was Mildred Kerr Bush (Millie). Millie was a pol's dream! Millie belonged to the only Republican who could challenge her popularity, Barbara Bush.

Millie's pups made the cover of *Life* magazine! The most popular book of the Bush presidency was *Millie's Book*, a

children's tale Millie "wrote." (The royalty check from
Millie's biography exceeded $900,000, about $899,000
more than George Bush's autobiography.) The proceeds
from *Millie's Book* went to charity.

A living symbol of domestic affairs! Women's issues!
"Kind and gentle" Millie!—all of the president's perceived
weaknesses.

But jeepers, George just didn't want that wimpy
mommy dog as *his* dog. The prez wanted a foreign-affairs
dog! A man's dog! A Dog of War! Bush never got the dog
thing: People love dogs, especially pols' dogs, because they
make us more *human*. Not more *animalistic*.

"Politicians generally need animals as a PR thing, a nice
thing; it redefines them as being more acceptable, more
compassionate," said Alan Beck, director of the Center for
Applied Ethology and Human-Animal Interaction at
Purdue University. "You see someone with an animal, you
attribute to them more qualities than they actually
deserve."

Yet Bush kept playing mean, junkyard-dog politics—
kept boasting, in 1988, he was mean as a "pit bull." Sent
Dan Quayle across the country snarling at Dukakis and
bragging he was the president's "pit bull." Nasty stuff.

Even Nixon knew better. Who can forget the veep nom-
inee in 1952 admitting on TV that he had accepted a spaniel as a gift from a wealthy California businessman—but his
kids loved that dog, Checkers, and the family was going to
keep it no matter what folks said. The public response
saved Nixon's career. Heck, even Patton allowed his terrier
to *soften* him.

Millie's symbolic fall came on February 23, 1991. Late
that evening, after consulting with Secretary of State
James A. Baker III, congressional leaders, the presidents

and prime ministers of seven other countries, and the four living former U.S. presidents—Reagan, Nixon, Ford, and Carter—Bush went on television to tell the nation he had ordered the ground war against Iraq.

Then, ringed by Secret Service guards, he left his advisers and the First Lady behind and went for a solitary nighttime walk around the south grounds of the White House with his dog.

Ranger. The Dog of War. "A strong male dog," the president called him when he wasn't gushing on about "my son" or "the love of my life." The dog the commander in chief of the United States summoned to live in the White House one month after Hussein invaded Kuwait. This is, of course, mere coincidence, as is the well-documented fact that leaders throughout history almost always enlist strong male dogs to follow them on Screaming Death Marches and that Ranger is also the name of the powerful aircraft carrier that rained horrid high-tech death on the Iraqis from the Persian Gulf.

That's all we'll say for now except that the companion the president turns to during global crises spends his days sniffing at his mother's private parts.

Ranger? Millie's two-year-old son.

(The Bushes, thanks to Spaniel Spin Control, received not a whimper of criticism for failing to neuter Millie, tacitly setting responsible dog ownership back twenty years, then actively doing the patently immoral thing, *breeding*.)

The prez coulda learned a thing from Schwarzkopf. After the war, the conquering general held a press conference and said he couldn't wait to get home. To hug his ol' dog.

Put a Mutt in the White House!

Given the troubling events during the Nixon, Ford, Carter, Reagan, Bush, and Clinton administrations, "Wild Things" urges you to put someone truly intelligent and trustworthy in the White House to represent fairly all Americans, i.e., a mutt.

We admit a bias. Ever since the president tried to buy an expensive purebred golden retriever, "Wild Things" has been pressuring the White House to adopt a mongrel from the dog pound.

There may be more important issues in the world, but there aren't many where the president could save millions of lives and millions of taxpayer dollars with one half hour of effort.

The *Los Angeles Times* has called this Washington scandal "Puppygate."

Roger Caras, president of the New York ASPCA, supports the Bill Clinton Adopt-a-Mutt campaign, as does the American Humane Association, Friends of Animals, the Doris Day Animal League, the Chicago Anti-Cruelty Society, the Los Angeles SPCA, and many other groups. More than five thousand Americans have added their voices so far. We are even receiving hate mail from golden retrievers.

Here's how you too can join the Bill Clinton Adopt-a-Mutt campaign. Simply mail your name, address, and signature to "Wild Things," P.O. Box 63, Riverton, New Jersey 08077. We will add your signature to the thousands being sent to the White House. If you're feeling ambitious, draw up a simple petition like the following, which is being circulated by shelters nationwide, circulate it among your friends, then send it to us.

We, the Undersigned Americans, Urge the President of the United States to Go to a Shelter and Adopt a Dog for the White House Because:

1. Millions of homeless mixed-breed and purebred dogs and cats are needlessly killed in the nation's animal shelters each year.

2. Millions of dollars in taxpayers' money is wasted on the slaughter of these perfectly good family pets.

3. The president's humane leadership would, in the words of the ASPCA's Roger Caras, save "hundreds of thousands of dogs who would otherwise be put to death but would now be adopted by homes who want to follow the White House example."

CHAPTER 5

YOUR HOUSE DOG THINGS

IN WHICH WE MEET AL HAIG HOUNDS,

MARQUIS DE SADE SHEPHERDS,

REVEAL WHY CANINES ARE SMARTER THAN CATS,

AND SPEND A NIGHT WITH FIVE HUNDRED DOGS

How Do Dominant Dogs Give the "Kiss of Death"?

The most terrifying human gesture we know of was delivered by Marlon Brando in *The Godfather*: the kiss of doom. Awful as this is, there remains *some* recourse: One can beg, grovel, hire one's own hit man, or (our favorite method of handling crisis) practice massive denial.

Compare this to the unalterable fear and complete belly-up submission that seizes a lowly dog when a Top Dog delivers *the look*.

The look, as you might imagine, is delivered with the

dog's eyes, which widen slightly yet somehow take on a hooded appearance as he glances across the room at your other dog, who quickly looks away.

Your dogs have been delivering murderous threats by glancing across the room and looking away for years now while you've been watching TV and commenting on how well they get along. Once you learn to recognize *the look* your dogs will start looking at you and looking away and you will feel like an American in Paris who suddenly speaks French after years of pointing—"Ah, ah"—to your mouth to indicate hunger. French waiters will always despise you, but your dogs will offer you a whole new respect.

I, for instance, believed that Daisy and Blue, our white dog and our black dog, coexisted happily like brother and sister. Actually, for seven years, their relationship was more like that of the Marquis de Sade and one of his chambermaids. I just hadn't noticed.

Then we built a family room.

The first night my wife, Jill, and I spent watching TV in the family room, Blue, our trusty fifty-pound black Lab mix, was afraid to enter the new room. This was astonishing because Blue never leaves Jill's side. It was also astonishing because Blue was afraid to cross an invisible line ten feet six inches from the threshold to the new room, as if the Cosa Nostra had painted the black hand in that exact spot, which, in a sense, it had. I called, "Here, Blue, c'mon, boy!" He refused to cross the invisible line. I put down my plate of spaghetti and meatballs on the floor and said, "Here, Blue." Blue didn't budge. I looked down at Daisy, our fifty-five-pound white shepherd mix, who smiled at me calmly, adoring as always. When Blue stepped into the room, she calmly glanced across the room at him and he swiftly retreated to a point ten feet six inches from the entrance to the new room.

Alarmed, I visited the anthropologist Elizabeth Marshall Thomas, who spent thirty years studying dog behavior and wrote the best-seller *The Hidden Life of Dogs*. Thomas told me, "This is perfectly normal. This is the most classic story of dog territorial dominance I have ever heard." I took this to mean, *I own the most dominant dog in history.*

Why me? What to do?

I called my friend, dog trainer Brian Kilcommons, who taught Diane Sawyer's Gordon setter, George, to stop knocking people over with bumps to their crotch. "You've lost control of your household," Brian said.

"Of course," Brian added, "this is normal. Male dogs almost always defer to females when they pull rank. People, too, in most households. But Daisy thinks it's her house now. She's deciding who gets to go into what room. It's time to remind her, 'Hey, babe, I pay the mortgage, not you.' "

Daisy is your typical "Alpha dog," or dominant dog. Dogs, like wolves, live in a complicated society where rank determines roles and helps the survival of the pack. Here's what do to when your Alpha dog attempts to become an Al Haig dog and tries to expand her power beyond reasonable bounds:

Detect invisible Alpha waves. After we realized that Daisy was giving Blue *the look*, years of odd behavior made sense. Blue standing ten feet six inches from his dog dish, afraid to eat. Blue refusing to chase a tennis ball, once his favorite sport. Other Alpha-dog dominance signals include sexless mounting; the spring-threat, which looks like play but is equal to *the look;* forward-pointing ears, raised back hair, and a low growl.

Just say no. When you see *the look,* Kilcommons says, simply say, sharply, "Cut it out!" Repeat as necessary. A dominant-submissive relationship is natural to your dogs, and healthy, but if it gets out of hand the Top Dog will keep bullying, "like a corporate honcho who realizes you can be pushed around. Then the nightmare really starts," Brian says. An unchecked Al Haig dog may get bigger ideas, like keeping *you* out of certain rooms or biting visitors.

"All these different threats remind the inferior dogs of the high status of the top dog," Desmond Morris writes in *Dogwatching.* "But he does not have to perform them very often. . . . It is essential that top dogs (or top wolves) are not too overbearing."

Why Do Dalmatians Always Ride on Fire Trucks in Fourth of July Parades?

As the "original, one-and-only coaching dog," guardian, and follower of horse-drawn vehicles, the Dalmatian had an ease around horses that made him the firehouse dog in the early days of horse-drawn fire fighting, says *The Complete Dog Book,* which was put together by the American Kennel Club. Now the Dalmatian's role as firehouse pet is purely symbolic, since many of these dogs are deaf and can't hear the bell.

What Is the "Heinz" Dog?

The "Heinz" is a Roaring Twenties synonym for *mutt*, now returning to fashion on dog walks everywhere, as in: Proud Dog Owner Number 1: "Even though we rescued him at the pound and he only cost seven dollars, we think Trooper is actually a purebred black lab"; or Dog Owner Number 2: "I don't know . . . looks like a Heinz to me."

Heinz as in "Heinz 57 Varieties," of course. The term entered the language in 1925, according to the *Dictionary of American Slang*, when founding patriarch H. J. Heinz was promoting his "Heinz 57 Varieties" slogan nationwide. By the way, Heinz simply *made up* the number 57 (there weren't then, and aren't now, exactly 57 Heinz products). According to a 1982 *American Heritage* magazine profile of Heinz, the founder chose 57 for "occult reasons."

The Heinz Company vociferously denies this. The official story is that 57 was just a catchy number to ol' H.J., who was not at all interested in devil worship. The whole matter is frankly a pain in the mutt for the Heinz Company, now an international food conglomerate also understandably eager to distance its popular mustard for hot dogs from confusion with other kinds of dogs.

"We hear about the 'Heinz 57 dog' all the time," sighed Beth Adams, a Heinz spokesperson in the Pittsburgh headquarters. "There's nothing we can do about it. Some things you can control, and some things you can't. This is in the public domain."

Where Can I Adopt a Berlin Wall Guard Dog?

Buy a piece of the Berlin Wall. Reread *Mein Kampf*. Listen to Wagner. Write a letter to Helmut Kohl. But no matter how intrigued you are by German history, *do not* adopt one of the Berlin Wall guard dogs, recently unemployed, that are being offered through American brokers.

The 220 German shepherds and Rottweilers that guarded the Wall were trained to behave in, well, *altered states*. Job Michael Evans, the New York celebrity dog trainer whose business name is The Patience of Job, urges extreme caution: "One of my clients, a wealthy lady on the Upper East Side, adopted one of the border sheps, and three weeks later she called me in a panic. The dog had divided the apartment into two sides and was menacingly pacing the border. Once she walked into the guest room—and there was the dog, growling, prohibiting her from ever going in that room again. Finally she scolded the dog for stealing a pizza that was cooling on the oven door—and the dog attacked her. When she locked herself in the bathroom it tried to rip the handle off the bathroom door."

It's more sensible, and humane, to adopt a dog from a German Shepherd Rescue Society. Your local dog shelter can give you the number of the rescue society in your area.

Why Do Dogs Hate a Man (or Woman) in Uniform?

This is a major national issue. Thirty percent of postal carriers lose time to their jobs from dog bites every year. About 2,500 to 3,000 are bitten seriously enough to warrant medical attention, says U.S. Postal Service spokesman

Marty Noble, "and yes, every now and then, we lose a postman." In 1986, a very bad year, with 4,000 bites, one Kansas City postman suffered a heart attack and needed 120 stitches after a dog attack.

Meter readers suffer even more bites. Utilities, post offices, and courier services spend hundreds of thousands of dollars on dog bite–prevention films, kits, and cayenne pepper sprays (carried by postmen). Dog bites are a major reason utilities are switching to electronic meter reading.

"Meter readers are even more invasive into the dog's territory than postal carriers, entering the house and basement," says Alan Beck, an expert on human-animal behaviors at Purdue University and a dog-bite consultant to the postal service.

Patti Anderson, a Federal Express courier in Mount Laurel, New Jersey, was delivering a copy of *The Hidden Life of Dogs* to the "Wild Things" household when Daisy, our gentle and loving fifty-five-pound shepherd mix, bit her on the boot. "All in a day's work," Patti said. "My wonderful family dog, Skipper, bit everyone who came to the yard in a uniform," she added. "Postmen. Meter readers. Garbagemen. My brother-in-law, but only when he wore his military uniform. I've been chased by dogs many times in my blue FedEx uniform, and my husband, who is also a FedEx courier, has a scar on his ankle from a dog bite. I mean, how do they know it's a uniform?"

Patti is also a marvelously courageous and patient person. Six months after saying the above, she was delivering yet another book to our house. Daisy sprang out the door and bit Patti on the foot. Appraised of the experts' thinking, that it was because she was a stranger to the house, Patti said, "Yeah, but my dogs never bit other strangers—only strangers in uniform."

Dogs are genetically programmed to defend the castle (*your* castle, buddy) from men in uniform just as they protected the ancient city from armies (more men in uniform), some experts theorize.

Says Beck, "This age-old thing with dogs and uniforms is probably apocryphal. Any stranger who came into your yard for a minute or two and left would probably have a high incidence of dog bites. Postal carriers don't hang around long enough so that the dog feels comfortable around them."

Keep your dog in the house when the postman rings, especially little dogs, who are expert at darting under the protective mailbag for ankle nips, and especially when school lets out and dog bites soar. Your dog, Beck says, "is basically a puppy wolf, protective of the family" and is more likely to attack to protect children in the yard.

The threatened postman is under government orders not to ring twice.

What Kind of Dog Runs the Iditarod? Can My Dog Do It?

I never thought my dog Blue, who is the well-known tennis-ball retriever type, could pull a sled 1,100 miles over Alaskan tundra, fighting 140-below temperatures and howling winds. But Rick Swenson, a five-time winner of the annual Iditarod dogsled race, told me the other day that Blue was just the type he looks for on his team.

"Any dog that likes to run can do it," Swenson said. "And mutts have more heart." This is encouraging news for all dogs in America because Blue is certainly a mutt, a very popular type of mutt found everywhere, and the one in your neighborhood is no doubt lifting his leg on your peace roses as you read this. When we picked Blue up at the pound for $7, the little card on his cage said, HOUSE-BROKEN: NO. TYPE: BLACK.

This makes him the ideal Iditarod dog. "We all use mutts. No one uses *breeds*," Swenson said, spitting out the word with distaste. Out of 1,200 dogs in the race, "I only know of one purebred, a Siberian husky on one of the French teams." This is a great Iditarod myth: Many people think the dogs are all Siberian huskies. Most years, there are more poodles racing than Siberian huskies! (A popular team of standard poodles was banned this year by the Iditarod rules committee for being, in effect, too wimpy.)

"Siberian huskies are a joke," snorts New York sled-dog breeder and geneticist Harris Dunlap. "They've been ruined." The Siberian husky is a purebred recognized by the American Kennel Club, or AKC. "AKC dogs are rubbish," Dunlap says. "Go buy ten AKC golden retrievers, and I'll go get ten dogs out of the pound—and my mutts will live longer, be healthier, and *destroy* your goldens in a sled-dog race."

This is because of what geneticists call "hybrid vigor." "If you breed two inbred lines together, you end up with superior traits," Dunlap said. "Hybrid vigor is what made America great," Dunlap says, referring, of course, to our wonderful country of mixed-breed humans, otherwise known as *"the melting pot."*

To breed a great sled dog, you usually start with an Alaskan husky, the hardy, forty-pound mix that served the Arctic Indians for centuries. After that, anything goes.

"I've got a lot of Border collie in my dogs because they love to run, are smart, and have great heart," Swenson says. "Also cocker spaniel, saluki, gazehound, Belgian sheepdog, German short-haired pointer. I know guys who mix in coonhounds, bird dogs, golden retrievers, Labs . . . it's so mixed up, no one knows what's in the dogs."

Blue would seem ideally qualified, being the product of at least fifty types of dogs himself. Dunlap doubts Blue would survive the Iditarod because his wavy retriever-collie–type coat is not thick enough. But I am certain he would flourish. Peering out from the starting line at Nome, Blue would lead the team, with great hybrid vigor, to the nearest house with large Oriental rugs, which he prefers to peace roses.

How Did the Rottweiler Become Cujo, Monster Dog?

One of the joys of being a pet columnist, aside from having dogs lick ice cream off your face, is to reveal that the latest Media Monster dog-of-choice of crack dealers and other macho bad guys is really very sweet and no danger to you at all *as long as you read this column.*

Oh, sure, whose heart hasn't been broken by the Horrible News items?

Horrible News Item Number 1: Four-year-old Oakland, California, girl dressed as Barney the dinosaur is mauled in twenty places in a church schoolyard by the pastor's Rottweiler.

Horrible News Item Number 2: A seven-year-old Philadelphia boy is shot by a police officer who is trying to kill the Rottweiler mauling the boy.

Horrible News Item Number 3: Four young sisters attacked by a Rottweiler are saved by neighbors throwing trash cans at the dog. "It looked like a lion tearing a zebra apart," one rescuer says.

But the problem, of course, is people, not dogs. "Rottweilers are the most wonderful dogs," says Muriel Freeman, legendary judge of Rottweilers on six continents and one of the authors of *The Complete Rottweiler*. "But in our violent society, people ought to just go buy a gun instead of a Rottweiler. Then when they use the gun they'll get the blame. When they use the dog, the dog gets the blame. The dog does what you train it to do."

While Congress debates gun control, "Wild Things" offers this guide to Rottweiler control:

Don't buy one! Boosted by the fame, and infamy, of movie and news-report exposure, the Rottweiler has soared from relative obscurity to the second most popular breed in America in the recent American Kennel Club rankings, behind only the Labrador retriever. To meet the demand, the dog is being poorly bred, bought by people who have no business owning one (any more than a twelve-year-old has any business driving a Lamborghini), and has been widely mistreated to enhance its aggressiveness. If you want a nice family dog, a Lab or retriever mix from the pound is a far better choice than this highly protective muscle-bound one-hundred-pound dog the Romans bred to help them form an empire.

"The Rottweiler takes tremendous discipline early on, from a very experienced dog person," warns trainer Brian Kilcommons. "I just got a call from a man whose mother was backed into a corner by a Rott, and all I could tell him was to put it to sleep. He was sobbing on the phone, telling me, 'I had no idea.' "

Plenty of smaller, softer dogs will bark and growl enough to keep the bad guys away, unless you're being pursued by Medellín cartel hit men, in which case you should immediately swallow this column, dye your hair purple, and move to another state.

Don't leave a Rott alone with strange kids. Carl, the wonderful Rottweiler of childrens' book fame, baby-sits while Mom isn't around, which makes a nice fantasy, but don't try this at home. Thor, a 121-pound Rottweiler, killed two-year-old Billy Sheppard in Hicksville, Long Island, in May 1993 while Billy was seated on a backyard swing at a neighbor's house. Rottweilers, Freeman said, may easily interpret a neighbor's screaming child as a threat to your child and "remove the perceived threat."

Don't be a Rott-en cynic. As horrible as these stories are, a well-bred, well-trained Rottweiler is a wonderful dog. "The dog is being bought by people who are not as smart as a Rottweiler, and the dog just takes over, sometimes for the good," Freeman said. During the 1989 San Francisco earthquake, a Rott named Reona, upon hearing the screams of a neighbor's epileptic five-year-old girl, leaped a fence, ran into the house, and shielded the girl with its body, saving the child's life as the dog took the blow of a falling microwave oven. Reona was named Ken-L-Ration's Dog Hero of the Year.

Why Do Dogs Eat Poops?

Yes, "Wild Things" takes on gross subjects that civilized pet books and columns routinely ignore because of our nation's Calvinist history that denies that *we're all animals.* We're not afraid! This is, in fact, a major national problem that reduces the productivity of American workers; i.e., it's one of the most common problems at the vet's office.

Here's the scoop:

Coprophagy is the highly technical euphemism for the behavior of dogs who eat feces. Feces is the mildly technical euphemism we'll keep using in this article. Nobody really knows why, but dogs routinely devour deer, rabbit, horse, cat, and sometimes their own feces.

The coprophagic dog will be checked for medical problems, nutritional deficiencies, obsessive-compulsive disorders, all rare. The vet may give you this helpful hint: A teaspoon of MSG in your cat's food will keep the dog out of the litter box.

Other than that, go home, be happy. Brood upon the likelihood that dogs evolved the ability to eat anything containing nutrients. It's one of the great mysteries.

Says Karen Overall of the University of Pennsylvania's veterinary college: "It's just bizarre. Most of the dogs that we see that eat stool—their skin isn't flaking, their eyes are clear, and they aren't showing any other sign of mineral deficiency. They just *like* it."

Can Children and Puppies Ever Get Along?

Today's topic is: Training children and puppies to get along peacefully and not bite each other. (Next week: While you're at it, why not end all war?)

Yes, this assumes you've ignored the advice of every living dog expert and bought your children a Christmas puppy.

To save your sanity and keep you from returning dogs and children to sender, "Wild Things" suggests you immediately *cease and desist calling your new dog "good girl," even if it is a girl dog.* Second, do not call your new puppy "good boy," even if it is a boy puppy.

The "Wild Things" staff made this mistake. For seven years we modulated our voice in a high, loving pitch and said, "Good girl, Daisy! I'm so proud of you!" whenever our girl did something laudable. Unfortunately our "girl" was a fifty-five-pound German shepherd mix. Then three years ago we brought another girl, Grace, home from the hospital, who differed from Daisy in that she was an actual human baby girl. Last September we proudly added Julia, another actual girl. Now when Grace shows Daddy her highly abstract nursery-school paintings, he exclaims in a high, loving voice, "Good girl! I'm so proud of you!" Daisy, our original "girl," of course thinks, "That's me!" and comes rushing over and knocks Grace out of the way, wagging her tail, grinning mindlessly and saying, "What'd-I-do? Let's-go-out, what'd-I-do? Make-me-a-ham-sandwich, what'd-I-do? Throw-me-a-stick"—the usual dog Mr. Subliminal routine.

Grace, displaced, pushes the dog away, and says, "No, Daisy. *YOU* can't talk to Daddy now. *I'm* talking to Daddy now." (Right now, you're probably wondering, How did this guy become a nationally syndicated pet columnist? Well, anyway, back to the story.) "That's competition and it shouldn't happen," says Brian Kilcommons, New York dog trainer and coauthor with his wife, Sarah Wilson, of the forthcoming *Childproofing Your Dog.* "There's more than enough love to go around for both of them." Let the dog hang around while you're feeding Baby; include your pet. And "call your girls girls and your dogs dogs." Herewith, some more ways to help children and dogs get along:

First, whether you, as a new dog owner, adopted a shelter dog or bought a purebred, you should be aware of the

unwritten guarantee that comes with all dogs: YOUR NEW CA-
NINE MODEL HAS BEEN PRODUCT-TESTED FOR 120 CENTURIES AND
WILL GIVE YOUR CHILDREN YEARS OF FAITHFUL, HAPPY SERVICE AND
PROTECTION IF YOU FOLLOW THE GOLDEN RETRIEVER RULE. This is
similar to the Golden Rule, but for dogs. "Don't let your
children do anything to the dog you wouldn't want them
to do to other children," Kilcommons says.

Relax, your dog is a good dog. The dog that growls at children is exceedingly rare, and usually it's the child's fault. If
your dog seems too aggressive, call in a professional
trainer, don't dump the dog. Most problems are solvable.
More likely your dog will respond to child aggression by
running and hiding. Dogs will love and protect children
and babies and guard them fiercely against evil strangers.
Dogs, unlike people, can tell good from evil in a whiff.
"The tragic kidnapping in Petaluma," Kilcommons says, "almost certainly wouldn't have happened if there was a dog
in the house."

Stop toddler terrorism. "The first thing to teach a three-
year-old," Kilcommons says, "is that the dog's tail and legs
are not handles." Establish boundaries, the same way you
forbid your child from touching the stove. No riding
"horsie." No poking eyes or ears. No jumping on sleeping
dogs. (The old adage "Let sleeping dogs lie" is useful.) Gentle pets on the head and ears are best. Toddlers' pets on
flank or stomach may turn into alarming squeezes. "Toddlers tend to get too involved," Kilcommons says. "Dogs,
like people, do not want their genitalia poked at."

Give puppy a time-out. Buy a metal crate or Vari-Kennel
(large dog size), available in pet stores. It's the puppy's secure home, with blanket and food. When the kid gets too
wild around the dog, give either one or both of them a
time-out. At eight, a responsible child can help feed, water,

walk, and housebreak the dog, with a parent along. If this seems like work, it is. "Your dog is like a child," Kilcommons says, "that never grows up."

Have Dogs Lost the Mantle of "America's Pet" to Cats?

Dogs are still the most popular pet (if you cook the numbers just right). Yes, dogs, not cats, are still America's number-one companion animal if you're counting households, according to a recent survey conducted for *Parade* magazine. Sure, cats are more numerous—57 million cats outnumber 52.5 million pet dogs in the U.S., but more households own dogs. Sixty-seven percent of Americans own at least one pet; 72 percent of those surveyed owned dogs; 49 percent owned cats.

Can Dogs Think?

I am happy to report that a thirty-year biological field study by one of our nation's leading animal experts has confirmed that you were right: *Dogs can think.* There is, to be honest, no scientific evidence for this. "But show me the scientific evidence," says Elizabeth Marshall Thomas, "that people can think." This is an excellent point, not diminished by the fact that Thomas was rolling around in bed being slobbered on by an Australian shepherd as she said it.

Elizabeth Marshall Thomas you will recognize as the now-famous author of *The Hidden Life of Dogs.* This is a fascinating book for which Thomas, an anthropologist and novelist who is in her sixties, ran with a dog pack, fled the dogcatcher, and dodged cars. Sigmund Freud asked, "What do women want?" and never came up with an answer. Thomas asked, "What do dogs want?" and spent thirty years and 100,000 hours watching her own eleven dogs.

"Wild Things" chatted with America's new Dog Lady in New York for a pleasant hour, during which Thomas never got off the floor with Misty and Pearl, her two pack-mates, except to hop on the bed with them and hug and kiss, confirming what "Wild Things" has always believed. *All creatures want most to lie in bed and be hugged and kissed.*

Also:

Dogs don't want to be our best friend. Cheer up; dogs think we are "excellent substitutes," Thomas says. But what dogs want most is "to be with other dogs," she says. To truly make your dog happy, let him choose his own mate, make children and grandchildren, and marvel as twelve to fifteen dogs form a wolf-style pack. Left completely to themselves, your very own dog pack will astonish your neighbors by digging a fifteen-foot pit in your backyard. If you let your dog be a dog, he will still come when called (unless he has anything better to do), and—we're not fabricating here— teach his puppies not to foul inside the house.

Dogs don't want food most. This is hard to believe for any- one who owns a dog like my dog Blue, an American chow-hound mix who will spend up to twelve hours in the kitchen staring up at a dressed turkey on the counter, at- tempting by apparent mind control to get it to slide onto the floor. But Thomas, riding a bicycle, followed Misha, a two-year-old husky, on his rounds for several years in a 130-square-mile area of suburban Boston and was terribly disappointed. Misha didn't want food, sex, or territory. He wanted to spend a pleasant day passing a little urine on permanent objects. He wanted, in wintertime, *his* pee to be highest on the snowbank. Yes, what dogs want most is *status*. (Suggested headline for this column: MAN'S BEST FRIEND COMPLETELY SHALLOW. Italic subhead: *only image counts*.) The truth is, image establishes rank and the resulting hierarchy is vital to the survival of the pack.

Dogs marry and divorce. Sound familiar? Dogs want what they can't have. Bingo, a one-eyed pug, was head-over-paws in love with Maria, a lovely husky, but Maria, predictably, was repulsed by the one-eyed pug and smitten with Misha, the handsome husky who peed higher on the snowbank than any dog in Boston. Maria and Misha fell wildly in love, had a grand romp, married, had four children (that's what Thomas called them), and shared "true romantic love," just like Romeo and Juliet. But the romance ended sadly. Misha had to move to another state, and Maria went into a major funk. "She lost her radiance and became depressed," Thomas writes.

Pugs are moral creatures. When Maria was harassing a cage of parakeets and mice, she was persuaded to behave by Bingo, the spurned, low-ranking, one-eyed pug, who crashed into the bigger husky, yelping in protest. Hurting the helpless, Bingo was telling Maria, was "morally wrong," Thomas says. Thomas also believes dogs are capable of amoral acts, such as rape, but that they would much rather choose their own sex partners.

Why Don't Canine Psychiatrists Dwell on a Dog's Early Years?

Let's be honest: Dogs are more interested in Kibbles 'N Bits than ego and id.

Dogs generally have happy childhoods. Unlike people, they don't fret over what their parents did to them.

"It seems that puppyhood in dogs is far less traumatic than puppyhood for people," says dog psychiatrist Karen Overall. "Puppyhood for dogs is much shorter than it is for people, and the scars that supposedly develop in people don't occur in dogs."

Whatever mysteries confound the canine soul, the dog shrink isn't interested.

"I don't know whether anyone has given any serious thought to penis envy in dogs," Overall remarks. "Why would they? It's not even valid in people. We're more interested in learning everything that goes on and behavior modification. You don't need to know what's causing the problem to deal with it."

So behaviorism is in, Freudianism out, at your local canine psychiatrist's. If your dog gets up on the couch, he'll probably be asked to get down.

Who's Smarter, Cats or Dogs?

Notice we didn't ask, "*Which* is smarter?" Dogs and cats are not a "which," dogs and cats are a "who." Because as any reader of "Wild Things" knows, pets are people too.

Animal behaviorists can't believe people wonder about this—it's perfectly obvious to them!

In the popular mind, cats have a higher intelligence and are crafty, choosy, manipulative, aloof. Dogs are slobbering, loyal, needy—qualities, in our Ironic Age, that aren't as cool. They just seem plain dumber. In fact, cats have very small brains; dogs' gray matter is much larger. Lots more neurons!

"In most of the tests, cats have not done as well as dogs," says Dr. Katherine Houpt, director of the Animal Behavior Clinic at Cornell University. "Part of the problem is that cats are less willing to work for food than dogs [in tests]. But how many cats can you teach to make six jumps and lie down and stay? Based on brain size, cats are probably not as smart."

How to Knit a Dog Sweater (a Real Afghan)

Today's pet lifestyle tip is: With only four shopping weeks left before Christmas, better start now if you're planning to knit Aunt Minnie a sweater from dog hair. Yes, "Wild Things" this week begins the first of several reports on Pet and Wildlife Gift Ideas with an economical, environmentally sensitive home project sure to delight every member of the family: *Knitting with Dog Hair*. This is the title of a book published by St. Martin's Press. We never make any of this stuff up. This fall, an internal memo was circulated at St. Martin's offices in New York: "Anyone with a dog, please save the hair for use as bookmarks. This is no joke!"

Authors Kendall Crolius and Ann Montgomery will show all Americans how to knit sweaters and bookmarks from the hairs that a white dog leaves on gray trousers. (Holiday etiquette tip: When Aunt Millie gushes, "It's a beautiful sweater! What kind is it?" *Do not under any circumstances admit the truth.* Just say, "It's an Afghan.")

"Wild Things" thinks knitting with dog hair is an excellent use of a wasted natural resource and, after all, Eskimos have done it for centuries. "It's not like skinning your cat to make a bath mat," Crolius points out. "You're harvesting what would normally end up clogging the vacuum cleaner."

Dog hair is indeed the leading export in our house. Blue, our fifty-pound shaggy black Lab mix, produces two large bagfuls of black hair each week simply by lying on the carpet in the family room. Every Friday my wife and I get down on our hands and knees and fill the plastic bags that frozen waffles come in with great tufts of black hair that never has any fleas except May through September.

Each Monday the garbagemen in our town cart two cubic feet of black dog hair to the landfill, which is now filled with mountains of dog hair that will last thousands of years. After twelve years as a professional journalist, it is dismayingly clear that the most tangible thing I am producing is black dog hair.

Instead, why not make a sweater! Sweaters from spaniels alone offer an infinite variety of colors and styles, such as the chocolate-colored American water spaniel and the two-toned Brittany.

Dog Fancy magazine has noted this important trend, which it calls "Chiengora Chic" (*chien* being the French word for "dog"). One Los Angeles woman spins yarn from her keeshond while the dog sleeps at her feet. Jean Pickles, a fourth-grade teacher from Chattanooga, Tennessee, knitted a hip-length, wrap-style jacket of muted tans and grays from the hair of her late collie, Satin. "It's a nice way to always have her with me," Pickles said, "and it doesn't itch like wool does." Dog-sweater wearers claim it feels as cozy as a heating pad and, most rewarding, *their dogs seem to know it's them.*

Here are some tips: Collect many bushels of dog hair and send it to a spinner who'll clean it and weave it into yarn. Flea powders and heavy dirt in the hair can pose health hazards. Discard any hair that has a lot of grass in it. *Knitting with Dog Hair* will provide tips on how to treat the fur so you won't smell like a wet dog when it rains.

Dog-yarn spinners prefer collies and other long-haired dogs whose fur has a slight crimp in it. Smooth fur from cockers and Maltese spaniels and Shih Tzus pulls apart too easily. Golden retrievers "come up lovely," dog-hair spinner Pam Gardner told London's *Daily Telegraph.* As a rule, the colors of the thread are less glowing than the colors of the living animal. Thus, black dog comes up gray and goldens show a pale yellow. "Persian cat is quite nice," Gardner said. "It's softer but not quite as strong as dog hair."

Dog hair produces some of the world's best wool, gushes Carol Gerke, who with Pam Scurlock runs a business in Grand Rapids, Michigan, called Hair Today, Yarn Tomorrow. Gerke will spin everything from camel to raccoon fur but, she says, dog hair "is smoother than regular wool, doesn't shrink or stretch, and it is incredibly warm."

Do Hotels Allow Dog Guests?

Yes. There are more suites available for Spot now than at any time in our nation's history. The American Hotel and Motel Association recently reported that 56 percent of its ten thousand members now accept dogs and cats.

Most of these lodges allow dogs in the room, on the bed, under the sheets, whatever your pleasure, pardner. If you're planning a vacation with Fido, "Wild Things" recommends the handy *Pets-R-Permitted Hotel & Motel Directory*, published by the Annenberg Communications Institute in Torrance, California. (See also page 119.)

Meanwhile many readers want to know where, in particular, they can stay with a dog in New York City while touring the Big Apple. This is easy. The most tolerant dog hotel in America is in New York City, where as many as five hundred dogs at a time spend the night. "Wild Things" personally investigated this.

Yes, after two nights in a hotel with five hundred dogs, "Wild Things" can heartily recommend the once grand Hotel Pennsylvania, unless of course you need actual sleep. Glenn Miller and Jimmy Dorsey started out there in their glory days, and now it's the Ramada Hotel Pennsylvania, right across from Madison Square Garden, that's gone to the, well, dogs.

The night we stayed there, the Westminster Kennel Club was putting on its famous show at the Garden, and the hotel was full. Six dogs to a room. We stayed up listening to pooches howl at the sirens of a New York night. We trod carefully on the sidewalks around the hotel, where Arnie, a yellow Labrador retriever from Texas, lifted his leg while a phalanx of hotel clerks advanced with garden hoses. The lobby was the place to sniff and be sniffed.

The maids refused to enter many of the rooms and went on strike. "It's very scary," a maid told us. "You don't know if a dog is in the room or not, and then you open the door and there it is!"

Every room needed six extra towels. "Slime rags," explained Susan Sword, a mastiff owner. "Have you seen these dogs drool? When they shake their heads, it's Look out! My maid back home says I have to get Rubbermaid wallpaper."

The Ramada staff really knows how to cater to a dog. (The second year the Westminster dogs came to the hotel, each dog was supplied with an adult sanitary napkin.) To book an evening with Fido, call (212) "PEnnsylvania 6-5000"—it's the old Glenn Miller song and still the hotel phone number.

CHAPTER 6

CELEBRITY
THINGS

IN WHICH SPUDS MCKENZIE IS SEXUALLY CONFUSED,
POE'S RAVEN IS FOUND IN A CLOSET IN PHILADELPHIA,
AND LETTERMAN'S DOGS DIE HORRIBLY

How Did Spuds McKenzie Die?

Yes, Spuds McKenzie, the most famous dog of the 1980s, that Reagan-era sex symbol, is dead. In this era of $2,000 cancer cures for dogs, even the finest pet dialysis treatment couldn't save the famed Anheuser-Busch party animal from succumbing to kidney disease.

Spuds died at his home in Riverside, Illinois. He was ten.

Make that, ah-hem, *she*. The macho sex symbol, always draped by the curvaceous Spudettes in Bud Light ads, turned out to be female.

"We were crushed," said Bud Light marketing director Bob Lachky, confirming the death. "Spuds was one of the most powerful advertising ideas in the last twenty-five years." Like Greta Garbo, Spuds lived reclusively in her final years and her death was shrouded in secrets, of which Spuds had many. Not only was Spuds not male, Spuds wasn't Spuds. Her real name was Honey Tree Evil Eye, Evie for short.

Evie actually died in the spring of '93, but owners Stan and Jackie Oles were so sick of reporters camping on their front lawn snooping out Spuds stories, they didn't inform a shocked and mournful world until autumn.

"Stan and Jackie are devastated," Judy Hamby (former editor of *Barks*, a bull terrier magazine) of Columbia, Illinois, told "Wild Things." "They would have done anything to save Evie."

This one's for thee, Evie.

Bob Dole Follows the Leader

"Wild Things" would like to put to rest vicious rumors emanating from the U.S. capital: Our Leader in Washington, D.C., has *not* been lost or kidnapped, nor is he currently involved in the type of sexual scandal that he has clearly enjoyed in the past.

Many politicians in our capital pretend to be leaders, but only one answers to the call "Here, Leader!" This is, of course, Senator Bob Dole's pet schnauzer, Leader, who once was embroiled in a controversy about his bed partners that would have put Wilbur Mills in a sweat. And once he did get hopelessly lost in the Capitol Rotunda and was heard barking uproariously, which apparently woke several congressmen. But lately Leader has not been hounded by bad press. "Leader is safe and sound and was in his bed in the senator's office yesterday," Senator Dole's press secretary, Clarkson Hine, told "Wild Things."

In fact, Leader is getting the kind of coverage a congressman would happily bark and roll over to receive. Yes, that was snarly little Leader you saw on "Good Morning America," being whisked to a meeting in the White House in the backseat of the Senate minority leader's sedan, with Dole and chauffeur in the front seat in deference to the dog, making insiders wonder, not for the first time, just who was the leader in the Dole household. That was Leader featured in a recent "60 Minutes" profile of Senator Dole.

Before this rash of coverage, Leader was best known for the press release he issued in 1990, on Senator Dole's stationery, coming to the defense of Millie, who had just been named the ugliest dog in Washington by *Washingtonian* magazine. The magazine's attack was "an arf-front to dogs everywhere," Leader was quoted as saying, and furthermore, the magazine's editors "had better watch their step."

Leader's new prominence raised grumbles among animal lovers recently at the American Humane Association's national convention in Baltimore. They agreed it would be terrible if the sexually charged little schnauzer became a role model for our country's dogs, especially since the Doles had promised to "fix" Leader and then let him out to stud. "It was pretty embarrassing for the Washington Humane Society when Leader got adopted," said Pat Heller of the Potter League for Animals in Middletown, Rhode Island.

Yes, the schnauzer was a gift from Bob's wife, Elizabeth, in 1988, after Dole was elected Senator minority leader. Dole quipped that the dog was "an indication where my leadership is going. Housebroken but not Senate-broken."

There were plenty of Beltway jokes about dogs resembling their owners and schnauzers being testy little things. But Senator Dole at least won points from animal activists for adopting the dog from the Washington Humane Society.

A representative for Senator Dole even signed the spay-neuter agreement, which turned out to be an election-year promise, i.e., a bald-faced lie. Yes, Senator and Mrs. Dole infuriated animal lovers in 1990 when they proudly introduced Leader's eight "power pups" in Senator Dole's office in a wicker basket under formal portraits of President Eisenhower and Pocahontas. This is literally true. The mom was Senator Strom Thurmond's schnauzer, Chelsea Marie. Senator Dole was apparently under the common misimpression that his manhood would be threatened by having Leader fixed. "Frankly," said a Dole spokesman, "the Doles had some concern about putting the dog through the neutering procedure."

Whatever Happened to Poe's Raven?

Poe's Raven actually belonged to Charles Dickens. And yes, the Raven lives . . . evermore. You could major in English Lit at Penn and never learn these essential things. The Raven was given as a gift to Dickens in 1840, when he was researching ravens for *Barnaby Rudge*. In 1841 Edgar Allan Poe, then a literary critic in Philadelphia, savaged Dickens's use of the raven in *Rudge*, saying a raven could be put to far better literary use. Poe began to write the immortal poem *The Raven*.

Meanwhile, a year later, Dickens's pet raven ate two pounds of white lead paint, "and this youthful indiscretion terminated in death," Dickens sadly wrote.

On the same day, twenty-nine years later, Dickens himself died. And the Raven—who had spent those twenty-nine years stuffed and mounted in a 27×25-inch glass case in Dickens's house—was sold and began almost a century of wandering through auction houses in New York and London. Finally, in 1951, the Raven was acquired in New York by Colonel Richard Gimbel of the department-store fortune, who upon his death in 1971 gave the Raven to the Free Library of Philadelphia, where the Raven remains today, locked in a closet in Philadelphia, next to a sign: THE MOST FAMOUS BIRD IN THE WORLD. Ask to see him in the Rare Book Department of the main library.

"The Raven is in much better shape than you'd expect of a creature 152 years old," said his restorer, Robert Peck. "He's in remarkably good condition. He has kind of a jaunty appearance. There's a slight cock to his head and a defiant attitude. It's humbling to see him. He's recently had some cigarette beetles—which feed on dead flesh—scraped off, was freeze-dried, and is expected to haunt the closet evermore. He'll outlast us all, unless you decide to be enclosed in a glass case."

Whatever Happened to Letterman's Dogs? (Or: Stupid Letterman Tricks)

Since we're reasonably certain at least *some* of the fourteen million readers of "Wild Things" overlap with David Letterman's three million viewers, "Wild Things" is investigating a very important question: Is it true that Letterman's beloved dogs, Bob and Stan, the longtime stars and inspiration for Letterman's most famous routines, were rewarded with horrible deaths?

The answer, alas, is yes.

Sadly, it's a fact that Bob died terribly in Malibu, while living with longtime Letterman cohabitant Merrill Markoe, creator of "Stupid Pet Tricks," while Letterman and Markoe were estranged.

Previous press accounts said simply that Bob died on August 24, 1988, "after a long illness." But in a recent *Rolling Stone* interview, Letterman said, "It turned out Bob was ridden with cancer. He had eaten a Prestolog, and as a result, his lungs were covered with tumors. But they give off a nicely colored flame if burned—very festive for the holidays."

In her book *What the Dogs Have Taught Me*, Markoe confirms that Bob devoured a Scrabble board, a Joseph Heller novel, and antique Christmas ornaments before he found the fatal Prestolog. "Where food was concerned," Markoe says, "Bob was a freethinker."

When news reached him that Stan had also died in Markoe's custody, Letterman says, "I sent her a note of condolence over the death of Stan—[acting] completely ignorant of the fact that her mother had passed away a year and a half earlier . . . with Stan, word came to us that he'd somehow eaten an entire ham. Oh, God . . . and it just killed him. Too much ham."

After all those years with Letterman, you'd think the dog would have been immune to ham.

"Merrill went away and the dog-sitter left out a big platter of ham," confirms Giulia Melucci, Markoe's publicist at Viking Books, "and the dog got a lethal overdose of ham."

Death by ham is an awful fate that all pet owners should be wary of.

New Jersey veterinarian Lisa Barber confirmed that

"dogs can and do die from eating too much ham—not from the ham, from the fat." Eating an excess of fat can cause an inflammation of the pancreas that causes digestive enzymes to misfire and can bring on vomiting, dehydration, and death. "Never give your dog a platter of sausages, fatty meat bones, and all the holiday trimmings," Barber says.

At press time, Letterman was unavailable for comment.

Canine Quiz: Match the People with Their Dogs
(*Answers on pages 103–04*)

Liberace	Gee-Gee
Emily Brontë	Breezy
Marilyn Monroe	Tigger
Prince Charles	Maf
Barry Manilow	Flossy
Barbara Walters	Keeper
Anne Brontë	*Sale Gosse* ("Naughty Brat," in French)
Dan Quayle	Baby Boy
Elizabeth Taylor	Bagel

Paul McCartney's Beetle Mania

Singer Paul McCartney, the noted vegetarian and English farmer, arrived in America in April 1993 on his world tour, "elated" over his recent victory in the biggest animal-rights war in years. This was, of course, the Test-Crash Offensive, in which General Motors suffered horrible public relations losses by admitting to being the only automaker that had killed twenty thousand dogs and other potentially nice family pets since 1981 and insisting it was necessary "for passenger safety."

These were ingenious experiments like crashing dogs into (a) hard steering wheels and (b) soft steering wheels, to see which did more damage. (Correct answer: *a*.) GM did, however, score a priceless PR coup when protesters in bunny, rat, and pig costumes pounded a 1985 Oldsmobile Cutlass with sledgehammers for half an hour but could not crack the body of the car. This was the best news to come out of Detroit in years. "Maybe it shows our cars are still built with quality," observed New York Olds district services manager Cannon Fears.

Helping lead the charge was McCartney, who is, of course, famous for such sayings as "I Want to Hold Your Hand" and "People are trying to deny that they are eating something that has a face, a heart, a soul."

Nowadays the handsome ex-Beatle has been embraced by a younger generation who all know him as a famous member of that internationally known group People for the Ethical Treatment of Animals (PETA).

Vegans and other fans, of course, know that the singer's wife, veggie-cookbook author Linda, is on record as saying, "I could never kiss a man who was a meat-eater," inspiring Paul to feed his road crew of 180 only vegetables. (McCartney reportedly gave his crew written warning they would lose their jobs if they so much as brought a bologna sandwich to work.)

When PETA's Heartbreak of America campaign began in 1991, GM officials watched in horror as McCartney helped lead thousands of people in boycotting GM cars. The actor Alec Baldwin joined in by refusing to be in a GM ad. Hollywood director Richard Donner did deliberately awful things to GM vehicles in *Lethal Weapon 3*, in which he also took shots at people who eat tuna-salad sandwiches.

In February GM agreed to put an end to the world's last animal test-crash experiments. PETA Washington, D.C., executive Dan Matthews—who rings up Paul and Linda regularly on the telephone to plot PETA test-crash offensives—called it "the biggest victory for animal rights since Revlon stopped animal testing for cosmetics."

GM admitted to slamming twenty pigs into steering columns to test liver damage, probing twenty-five ferret brains with power drills to test cortex damage, and pounding a dozen dogs' hearts with an air-driven metal disc. GM spokesman Jack Dinan said animal research played a large part in GM's development of crash dummies that now will save animal lives.

When McCartney kicks off his American tour April 14 in Las Vegas, fans will make their way past PETA protest tables, hear Paul sing an animal-rights anthem, "Looking for Change," and see a full-page PETA ad in the program. GM wanted to buy a full-page ad in the program, but a horrified McCartney "pulled their ad and gave the page to PETA," said Paul's spokesman, Joe Dera.

Mozart's Starling

Yes, it's one of the more touching moments in pet history: On May 27, 1784, Wolfgang Amadeus Mozart gave his heart to a starling, the pesty bird that most people in the twentieth century fantasize about killing.

There are 200 million starlings in our great country today, most of them sitting on telephone wires, and that's 200 million too many in the opinion of many utilities and municipalities spending taxpayers' money to poison the speckled pests.

Mozart saw it differently. Three years after he bought the bird, Mozart buried his pet with great ceremony as veiled mourners marched in procession, sang hymns, and wept as the composer read the kind of touching poem that makes us glad he kept his day job.

> A little fool lies here
> Whom I held dear—
> A starling in the prime
> Of his brief time
> Whose doom it was to drain
> Death's bitter pain
> Thinking of this, my heart
> Is riven apart . . .

In our own time, scholars have interpreted Mozart's love for a widely despised bird as a sign of the composer's mental deterioration. But Meredith J. West, editor of the journal *Animal Behaviour*, says the critics miss the point. The starling, in fact, is a wonderful pet. The small, black, white-star-splashed birds are brilliant mimics that copy cat meows and dog barks and make great pets at a fraction of a parrot's cost. West's pet starling often asks, "Does Hammacher Schlemmer have an 800 number?" Meredith's starling has watched so much college basketball that whenever the TV is on, he chants, "Defense! Defense!"

What Did William Wegman Do Before Dog Photographs?

Once upon a time, Wegman was a young artist who proclaimed that painting was dead. He wrote a car concert for honking horns, and folks covered their ears. He floated a 250-foot chain of Styrofoam commas down the Milwaukee River, and people scratched their heads. He was, he admits, becoming increasingly "pompous" and no doubt destined for obscurity.

Wegman went to art school in Boston in the sixties and did so much coke and alcohol that his first wife, Gayle, left him. But not before she bought him the puppy Man Ray, whom Wegman named for the pioneering American surrealist, for $35. In 1972 Wegman moved with Man Ray to New York City and by the late seventies was doing giant Polaroids of the dog. Today, of course, Wegman, forty-nine, is a rich and famous artist, thanks to Man Ray, easily the most celebrated dog in twentieth-century art.

Cat Dishing

According to the magazine *250 Fabulous Cats and Stars Who Cherish Them*, Whitney Houston dropped $5,000 on diamond collars for her two Persians. Actress Mary Frann's cat, Stolichnaya, stars on soap operas. Rue McClanahan made a cat-care video, and "Dynasty" star Linda Evans has a Siamese creatively named She.

Who Was the Most Beloved Dog in History?

This is a ludicrously subjective choice, but that's the nature of "Wild Things." Send us your nominations for better-loved dogs and we'll apply the same grossly subjective standards and *your dog, too,* could become an immortal. Meanwhile read about Flush and weep.

Flush was Elizabeth Barrett Browning's dog. If anyone ever needed a dog, it was Elizabeth Barrett. She was a virtual prisoner in her room in London in the 1840s, a semi-invalid confined to a couch, reading classic Greek authors and writing poetry. Her lone companion was her domineering father, Edward Moulton Barrett, who discouraged visitors, suitors, and all attempts by Elizabeth to *Get a Life.*

Enter Flush, aka Flushie, a gift from a friend. Flushie slept on Elizabeth's bed, ate sweet cakes from her hand, listened wide-eyed to her whispered rhymes, growled when she exclaimed anything to be beautiful but him.

Now we bring you an excerpt from the 120-line love poem "To Flush, My Dog":

> Yet, my pretty, sportive friend,
> Little is 't to such an end
>   That I praise thy rareness;
> Other dogs may be thy peers
> Haply in these drooping ears
>   And this glossy fairness.
>
>
> But of *thee* it shall be said,
> This dog watched beside a bed
>   Day and night unweary,
> Watched within a curtained room

> Where no sunbeam brake the gloom
> Round the sick and dreary.

When the poet Robert Browning came courting Elizabeth in May 1846—the very first meeting of their romance for the ages—Flushie bit his boot. Where a lesser man might have been angered, Browning, a genius, heartily agreed when Elizabeth said she couldn't imagine eloping to Italy without Flushie.

So it was that the three immortals—Browning, Barrett, and Flushie—lived out their days in sunny Italy, where Flushie remained forever "satisfied / If a pale thin hand would glide / Down his dewlaps sloping, / Which he pushed his nose within / After,—platforming his chin / On the palm left open."

Zsa Zsa's Heart Is Full of Shih Tzus

The "Wild Things" staff once was thrown out of a limousine in Miami by Eva Gabor after interviewing the buxom actress. Or was it Zsa Zsa? We forget. In any case, in 1993 Zsa Zsa, a real dog lover, was cruising on a Los Angeles freeway when she saw a Shih Tzu stranded on a median strip on the busiest road in the world. Her heart went out to the dog.

As you probably know, Zsa Zsa owns two Shih Tzus herself and will go to extraordinary lengths to prove her love for these dogs, whose names are Genghis Khan and Macho Man. (Hitler and Killer apparently were already taken.)

Genghis and Macho travel first-class with their starlet-celeb owner. According to *People* magazine, on January 30, 1989, Zsa Zsa was so adamant that her two pooches not be kept in those horrible eensy-weensie travel kennels on a

Delta Air Lines flight that police in Atlanta finally escorted the yappy little dogs off the plane.

So four years later, when she saw a Shih Tzu stranded perilously in the middle of one of the world's busiest highways, Zsa Zsa was naturally concerned. She stopped the car and shooed the dog across the street.

Answers to Canine Quiz:

Baby Boy: A French poodle, one of Liberace's twenty-one dogs, adopted and nursed from the brink of death by Liberace, according to Lynne M. Hamer's *Name That Dog.* Liberace's dogs thrilled to the sound of his voice over the telephone.

Bagel: A beagle owned by Barry Manilow, the cream-cheesy crooner.

Breezy: A black Labrador given to Vice President Dan Quayle by Duayne Allen of the Oak Ridge Boys. Name helps reinforce the vice president's penetrating intellectual style.

Flossy: Anne Brontë's black-and-white spaniel, who shared table scraps with Keeper.

Gee-Gee: What Elizabeth Taylor says when the minister asks, "Do you take this man as your lawfully wedded husband, to have and to hold, through sickness and health, for richer or poorer, so help you God?" Also the name of Taylor's poodle during her marriage to Michael Wilding.

Keeper: Emily Brontë's mastiff, who shared table scraps with Flossy.

Maf: Marilyn Monroe's dog, a gift from Frank Sinatra, who apparently wanted to impress her with his powerful friends.

Sale Gosse: A poodle owned by Barbara Walters.

Tigger: A Jack Russell terrier owned by Prince Charles. One of her puppies, born in 1988, was named Roo. We expect the birth of Winnie-the-Pooh any day now.

CHAPTER 7

PAMPERED PET THINGS

IN WHICH AMERICANS SPEND MORE MONEY AND LOVE
ON THEIR PETS THAN ON THEIR GRANDCHILDREN,
SPOUSES, MOVIES, AND VIDEOS
AND IN WHICH A CAT RIDES IN A ROLLS-ROYCE

What Can I Get the Pet Who Has Everything?

This is particularly useful for birthdays and holidays, when Americans fawn over their most beloved family members, who are, of course, cats, dogs, birds, hamsters, and even emotionless food-chain machines like snakes. Since our nation lavishes more fun money on its pets than on movies, videos, children, and grandchildren, "Wild Things" brings you a list of useful last-minute pet gifts, as well as completely frivolous trinkets you'll never be able to afford because you are not Ivana Trump (unless, perhaps, you keep saving and coming back, like Shirley MacLaine).

Luxe pet gifts, like fine restaurants, come in several distinct categories:

"Reserve the usual table at the Four Seasons, Chapman, and keep the limo warm." These are four-star pet gifts, and if you have to ask how much, darling, you're not a customer at Karen's For People Plus Pets at 1195 Lexington Avenue, New York City. Yes, you're likely to see Ivana here, buying completely frivolous things for Chappy, her toy poodle, and a Yorkie whose name was unavailable to us at press time but who we are certain is not named Marla Honey. Such as an alligator-leather dog-collar-and-leash set ($600). Or the Ralph Lauren Russian coat for dogs, a hand-knit red wool with black faux-lamb-trim number designed by Karen herself (up to $120, depending on size).

Or the Pet Children beds, made exclusively for this shop—a "good, sturdy, sensible custom bed" for dogs, says manager Carol Nolan, "with faux-down comforter and custom sheets." Life's cruelest choices are mahogany stain or white wicker frame? English Country or French high-style fabrics? "People bring their decorators in to make these choices. You have to know what room to put it in," Nolan says. "Don't make us sound like a pet shop just for the wealthy," she adds. "We have people coming in from Paris and Rome, too." No 800 number. No catalogue. Call (212) 472-9440, if you dare. A rival New York pet shop, Le Chien Pet Salon, has items such as an $8,000 dog necklace, Nolan states.

"Is this your best table, next to the men's-room door? It's my fiancée's birthday." Okay, so you're not recognized at the finest restaurants, but they'll take your name and seat you at ten-thirty. You're willing to spend a buck or two on your pet or pet owner, for practical value. Try such three-star

gifts as Wanderer Pet Luggage. Ross Becker, editor of *Good Dog!*, a consumer magazine for dog owners, recommends this "really nice suitcase for traveling with dogs. It's made of ballistic nylon with plastic water bottles and nontip bowls. Everything you need for dog shows or vacations." Call Deb Wand, owner of the Minnesota manufacturer, at (612) 688-7001. For new or misbehaving dogs, a wise investment is *Good Owners, Great Dogs*, an instant classic by New York dog trainer Brian Kilcommons and his wife, Sarah Wilson. (Call 1-800-457-PETS to order the $19.95 video.)

"Don't worry, honey. With only three cars ahead of us, the fries will still be warm." Sometimes the best things in life are cheap. Like Kitty Bird, a cat toy that Becker endorses and only costs $3–4. It's a small toy weighted with sawdust, sort of like a badminton cock, with nontoxic dyed turkey feathers on top. "My cat Cocoa loves to play fetch with me," Becker says, "I being the one who has to fetch." Call Kitty Bird, Inc., Deerfield Beach, Florida, 1-800-23-KITTY. *Good Dog!* is an excellent, colorful gift for dog lovers who want the latest product testing and canine health and food info. It's $18 for six issues a year. (Call 1-800-968-1738.)

"The fifty-pepper chili is fab, but can we move away from the kitchen exhaust vent?" If eliminating foul odors is your dream, consider the hot new odorless litter box named, yes, the Sweet P Cat, which filters cat pee through apoxy-coated pebbles down to a lower-level disposable diaper, which absorbs the urine without odor. Poops dry quickly on the pebbles and are scooped into a poop holder attached to one side. All this works very well, Becker says. Call the Sweet P Corp., 1-800-937-9909. For you pets and owners with "doggie breath," Oxyfresh USA Inc. markets

special drops for animal drinking water, and mouth rinse for humans, to stop halitosis. For an Oxyfresh representative, call 1-800-22-FRESH.

"Mom's out of town, kids, so it's dinner at the ice-cream parlor!" For completely fun, non-nutritious gift-giving, there's always the ever-popular Moose Drop Jewelry—odor-free earrings and key rings made from lacquered moose dung, from Maine Line Products in Portland, Maine. Or Frisbee Dog Treats. These wheat–corn starch–vegetable oil Frisbees (sort of like Frisbee ice-cream cones), alas, were abandoned by a major manufacturer after a failed Boston test marketing, Becker says. They kept breaking before Fido got his teeth around them.

How Can I Properly Bury My Beloved Pet?

America is gaining a decidedly competitive edge over Japan because of the growing popularity of pet burials, which are vitally important to all Americans, especially in September, which is National Pet Memorial Month. More and more Americans are burying their pets in cemeteries because most suburbs and cities forbid backyard burials and, as the *Chicago Tribune* has noted, "Pets are people too."

This is literally true in Japan, where Buddhist monks believe dogs and cats may be people in a future life and therefore monks get paid many yen to pray at pet gravesites. This is causing a national controversy in Tokyo, where residents are objecting to a proposed six-story downtown pet mausoleum because it would bring very bad luck unless proper spiritual care is taken of the animals' souls; if it isn't, the animals come back as American tourists. Anyway, no nation on earth dotes on puppies like our fine nation, where the newest trend is *being buried alongside your pet*. This is, of course, after you die, although "Wild Things" knows of a California couple who've already bought eight spaces in a pet memorial park—two for husband and wife and six for their dogs. Pet-person burials are usually preceded by cremation; man and critter are laid side by side in separate caskets. In very unusual places like Ohio, however, some persons are buried with their pets' ashes right in the casket, such as the Chihuahua and person interred together at Paws Awhile Pet Memorial Park & Crematory in Richfield. *Special warning to bereaved pet owners:* "No pet burial goes off without crying people," warns a grave digger at the Konik Nowy pet cemetery near Warsaw, Poland, where almost nobody can afford a coffin and a basket burial goes for the outrageous sum of 270,000 zlotys. So before you buy, consider carefully:

Your zlotys. You can easily spend many zlotys, say, $500–1,000 burying a pet. This includes an engraved headstone, a visit to the crematorium and viewing room, annual maintenance or perpetual-care fees, and, of course, a silk-lined pink or almond plastic Hoegh casket that looks approximately like a woman's traveling cosmetic case and, according to scientists at the University of Michigan, will last ten thousand years. Or you can do a simple cremation for well under $100.

Your emotions. After the owners of the Long Island Pet Cemetery were fined and jailed in 1991 for dumping 250,000 pets in a mass grave, Joyce Walp, forty-five, and Michael Bachman, thirty-six, dug up the grave of Ruffian, their ten-year-old sheepdog, which caused them to seek psychological counseling, especially because the grave was empty. Mr. Bachman got so upset he lost sixty pounds. The couple sued for emotional distress and was awarded

$1.2 million, to which *Newsday* editorialized, DOWN, JUDGE! DOWN! A good pet cemetery should be at least five acres and be dedicated and well maintained. Call the International Association for Pet Cemeteries at 1-800-952-5541 if you have any doubts.

Callous coworkers. "Wild Things" readers aside, there are in this fine newspaper's circulation area a few insensitive petless louts who will snicker when you say, "I just spent a thousand bucks to bury Spot" and start to cry. Just tell them, "Hey, buddy, that's what it costs." John Wayne gave *his* German shepherd a proper burial in Huntington Beach, California, near Karen Carpenter's dogs and José Feliciano's goat.

You're not alone. Twenty years ago everyone laughed at "pet cemetarians." Now there are 675 registered by the International Association. And 20 percent of the nation's pet owners pay for formal burials in a cemetery, says Widener University folklorist J. Joseph Edgette, an expert on this very subject. "Pets are a part of the family who stay with their owners for twelve years, through thick and thin," Edgette says. "After growing so close, owners aren't going to throw their animals in a trash can."

Who Do You Love More, Your Dog or Your Husband?

Ten thousand Americans were recently asked this very important question, and an alarming majority—58 percent—said they would get rid of their spouse if the spouse were allergic to their cat or dog. (Okay, this is assuming they'd just met their future spouse, but it's alarming just the same.) This doesn't surprise us. (That's why we thought of this piece!) Nor does the fact that 70 percent of dog owners and 62 percent of cat owners would give up their own lives to save their pets. And that 17 percent of dog and cat owners would pay any ransom—well over $1,000—to get their pets back. And that 60 percent of us allow our pets to sleep in the same bed with us and more than 70 percent wrap doggie and kitty birthday and Christmas presents. Asked whom they loved best, the majority ranked as follows: children, Mom and Dad, pets, siblings, bosses, and in-laws, according to Barry Sinrod, author of *Do You Do It When Your Pet's in the Room*?

Who Are the Most Pampered Dogs in the United States?

Notice we said "who" rather than "what." If you think pets are "whats" and not "whos" and therefore *not people too*, please give this book to a more highly evolved person. Meanwhile we nominate three salukis, which are actual purebred dogs, owned by Sandra and Michael Wornum of Larkspur, California. The salukis do not live in a typical doghouse. They dwell in their own $10,000 four-room addition to their masters' house. The "doghouse" features a bathtub, Erté lithographs, rugs from Istanbul, and portraits of the salukis themselves in the art gallery. Then, of course, there is the "repose room" for those days the salukis don't feel like getting out of their beds, Sandra Wornum told *Time* magazine. "If we have a dog that's ill or depressed or out of sorts for the day, we send him into the repose room and he gets himself back together," she said.

Why Isn't There a Twenty-Four-Hour Global Pet Channel?

Welcome to our occasional special program, "Pet Headline News," which differs from "CNN Headline News" in that it reports truly important developments, such as advances in cat litter, in less than three minutes.

In today's headlines: Eight percent of Americans continue to eat from plates their pets have licked. . . . Who *really* walks the dog and cleans the cat litter? . . . Birds are smarter than human beings in many respects and practice a keenly intelligent form of "the joy of sex," a researcher finds. . . . Little-known life-threatening cat diseases . . .

A look behind the headlines.

When Kids Say, "I'll Take Care of Him," Skepticism Is Advised

Yes, the classic line "I'll walk him, play with him, *pleeeeease* can't we take him home?" is just that: a line. According to a survey of 1,100 pet owners in thirty-five states conducted by the American Animal Hospital Association, 63 percent of those polled said the female head of household took care of the family pet. Male heads of households came in a distant second at 19 percent, and the promise-makers (sons and daughters) did the dirty work in only 7 percent of households surveyed.

Birds are better navigators than we are. Many of our Important Scientists maintain that animals have neither intelligence nor consciousness. This is the kind of thinking that is challenged in a fascinating book, *The Human Nature of*

Birds. Author Theodore Xenophon Barber reports that scientists have proven that birds can make and use tools; recognize and work with abstract concepts; show grief, joy, compassion, and even altruism; create complex musical compositions; perform intricate mathematical calculations in navigation; and even form true friendships with human beings. Birds also use intelligence to cope flexibly with changing life demands, and they play joyfully and mate erotically.

Eighty-one percent of cat owners kiss their kitties. Yes, and 48 percent of pet owners sneak their animals scraps from the table, and 41 percent feed them directly from their plates. Only 8 percent, however, continue to eat from a plate their pets have licked. (Please write us with details if you do this.) So says pet researcher Barry Sinrod. Watch Kitty for FIP and FIV. Most cat owners have heard of feline leukemia, the number-one infectious killer of cats. But owners need to be more aware of killers number two and three: feline infectious peritonitis (FIP) and feline immunodeficiency virus (FIV). About 500,000 cats die each year from the almost-always fatal FIV, but the good news is that veterinarians finally have a vaccine to protect cats from the disease, says Roy Pollock of SmithKline Beecham's animal health division. FIV is called "Cat AIDS" because it mimics human HIV (but is not infectious to humans). Screen any new cat for the fatal FIV virus before introducing him or her into your household. It's transmitted by bites between cats.

Is It True that Dogs Use Eau de Parfum?

Yes. This is what the world is coming to: For the pet (or owner) who has everything, Lisa Gilford, owner of Le Chien pet salon in New York City, has something more. Her customers, such as Precious, Peach, and Angel, the dogs owned by the *very social* Carol Petre, and Flo and Leo, Calvin and Kelly Klein's dogs, enjoy the fresh scent of Martine and Christophe—the first fine perfumes for dogs, 3.3 ounces in lovely French crystal bottles ($35 and $30, respectively).

"Christophe is for male dogs and is very woodsy," Gilford says. "Martine is for female dogs and is very feminine, with jasmine and such. It's nice after you've walked the dog in the dew or dirty streets to brush him and freshen him up with a little spritz."

Dog perfumes are very popular on Valentine's Day, as are dogs that weigh less than a box of chocolates. "People come in and buy a Maltese, a Yorkshire, or a French poodle," for their Valentine's Day beau, she says.

If you're buying perfume, lotions, or soap for a human, the Humane Society of the United States asks "that you spare a little affection for the animals and use cosmetics and personal-care products that are not tested on animals." Products marked "Beautiful Choice" are endorsed as cruelty-free by HSUS, are offered by almost thirty manufacturers, and are supported by celebs such as Trisha Yearwood and Woody Harrelson.

Whom Do You Love More, Your Grandchild or Your Cat?

As if we didn't spoil our pets enough, now comes news that America's grandparents spend more money on their cats, dogs, and other pets than they spend on their grandchildren! According to Strategic Directions Group, a Minneapolis marketing firm, grandparents spend an average of $48.81 every three months on their pets—and $43.92 on their grandchildren. Sometimes a dog's life ain't so bad.

What Can I Get the Cat Who Has Everything? (More Shameless Pet Gifts)

During the holiday season of light, millions of Americans ask the Big Questions: How can all of humankind find peace on Earth? And what can I get, as an individual, for the cat who has everything? After carefully analyzing *The Crazy Lady Cat Catalog*, "Wild Things" feels better prepared, for the time being, to address the latter question. Herewith the "Wild Things" Pet and Wildlife Holiday Gift Guide for all animal lovers, from the environmentally aware to deliciously cat-spicuous consumers.

Sip sweet mousecatel. For those long, lazy nights in front of the fire, what kitty could live without Fabio's Mouse-Skin Rug? Yes, this "sensuous, softly padded, faux mouse-skin rug" will "tickle the hairy little hedonist's fancy," *The Crazy Cat Lady Catalog* purrs. Picture a bearskin rug, only smaller, with rhinestone eyes and "a chic gold-trimmed pearl button nose." For only $49! Call us decadent and weak, but don't you just love catalog writing?

Of course, no New Year's Eve would be complete without a bottle of fine, vintage Catnip Mousecatel (eight-ounce bottle for $7), a perfectly *won*derful complement to Chocolate Catnip Petit Fours (three catnip-scented toys served on a paper doily, $10). For kosher kitties there's also a cat yarmulke ($8). This is all true. You can look it up (and order it from the Crazy Cat Lady at 1-800-282-MEOW).

Make PC pals howl. For the enviro-eco-sensitive, the National Wildlife Federation holiday gift catalog (1-800-432-6564) features seventy pages of gifts that help endangered species, such as the Wolf Pup Surprise momma-and-pups plush figures ($29.95) and the hand-knit Wolf Cardigan ($120). For a mere $20, you can Adopt a Whale for your child, support a coastal network to help stranded whales, and get adoption certificate, photo, decal, and quarterly updates on your whale. Or simply munch away on chocolate-covered rain-forest Brazil nuts. For $16.95, this helps save dwindling critters in the rain forest by supporting the hand-picking Brazil nut industry, a reason even a capitalist can love for not cutting down all those trees.

Penny-wise pampering. Who needs fancy catalogs when you've got a Caldor's nearby? The $19.99 Cat Napper is a rug-covered shelf that attaches to a windowsill so your cat can nap and look out the window at birds it dreams of eating. It's the perfect gift for cats, who sleep away 67 percent of their lives anyway. Caldor's $4.99 NFL Dog Sweater looks like a bargain compared to more costly catalog sweaters. Your have your choice of eight teams, including the Cowboys, Raiders, and Giants.

Ho-ho-ho humanely. The Humane Society of the United States has licensing agreements with several manufacturers through which a portion of their profits will benefit HSUS.

They include Steven Krauss Menswear Ties (a new line features all types of animal prints); Day Dream Calendars, with cat and dog photos; and Eagle's Eye women's clothing, with animal patterns. Look for the HSUS "Beautiful Choice" logo on cosmetic and personal-care products not tested on animals. Call (301) 258-3049 to receive an HSUS gift catalog.

Videos for cats and dogs. "Happy Tails," a video for dogs, features thirty minutes of "sights and sounds dogs love to watch," such as birds, pigs, cats, dogs, and even a trip to the vet. The suggested retail price is $19.99, says *Pet Age* magazine. Write to Happy Tails, P.O. Box 55071, Willowdale, Ontario, M2J 5B9, Canada. "Video Catnip" is a video filled with birds, squirrels, chipmunks, and nature sounds that will have your cat running and jumping toward your TV screen. To order for about $20, call Pet Avision, 1-800-822-2988. The sounds may briefly amuse you or your pets, but the fact is cats and dogs are generally bored with TV, scientists say, because the two-dimensional figures are too small for them to see, and dogs and cats respond to smell, not sight, anyway. Smear old leftovers on the screen and your dog will watch taped replays of congresspersons discussing NAFTA on C-SPAN.

What Can I Get the Dog Who Already Has a Silver Spoon?

Here's a stocking stuffer for oh-so-spoiled Spot. Alan Lilly, a former space-systems engineer in Orlando, Florida, figured the worst part of owning a dog was cleaning the spoon that scooped the dog food. So he designed a spoon that is eaten by the dog after scooping the wet food out of the can. What would our civilization be without an edible dog spoon? The product, Dog Spoonz, has gone over well with dogs, as does, of course, any organic matter that falls on the floor.

How Can I Take the Perfect Pet Photograph?

Use a high-speed film, such as ASA 400, to freeze movement, advises Linda Solomon of the Photography Information Council. Try to capture your pet in a spontaneous moment in his natural environment. Make embarrassing clucking noises and reward him with a snack to get a funny face. Focus on the nose and whiskers of cats and dogs rather than the eyes. Grovel down on the floor to shoot puppies, kittens, or small animals at their level. Avoid red-eye by taking the photo when your pet is looking away from the camera. All in all, pretend your pet is your child, Solomon says. (This is second nature for "Wild Things" readers, who have to try hard to imagine that their pet is *not* their child.)

Should the Jet-Setting Cat, When Flying to Paris, Take a Litter Box Aboard the Concorde?

These are the kinds of questions that haunt "Wild Things." In search of an answer, we recently interviewed Norton, the world's most accomplished pet traveler, at the Four Seasons Hotel in Philadelphia.

Norton often takes the Concorde to Paris, where he dates beautiful women, dines in five-star restaurants, hangs out with Roman Polanski and Harrison Ford, and, even more impressive, flies to Europe without *once* using a litter box.

Norton is, of course, a cat and the star of Peter Gethers's charming book, *The Cat Who Went to Paris* (the Ballantine Books paperback is easiest to travel with). A handsome Scottish Fold, Norton sat in the lobby darting his alarming green eyes nervously and sharing his utmost travel secrets:

Travel with litter. This is Gethers's favorite tip: "A five-pound litter bag fits in any decent suitcase," says Gethers, who packs two, "along with ten fold-up cardboard litter boxes." Journeying to France for a few weeks, Gethers restricts Norton's food and drink before takeoff so the cat doesn't have to go (except to Paris) during the six-hour flight. As soon as the jet lands in Paris, Gethers pops a litter box behind the taxi driver's seat and Norton is, well, relieved to be in Paris. Another litter box goes in the rental-car backseat, another in the villa in the south of France. Presto! Norton is ready for three weeks of foie gras.

Order from the pet menu. Yes, the Four Seasons in Boston has a room-service menu for pets, mostly dogs. Favorites include (a) Ruff, ruff, rrrrrr: broiled beef filet with natural broth, $6; and (b) Aohowww, aohowww, aohowwwwww: boneless lamb chops, $7. Entrées for birds? "There's nothing on the menu, sir," a hotel employee said, "but if we knew in advance you were coming with a bird, I'm certain we could arrange something." More and more hotels accommodate pets nowadays. Two of the best directories of those that do are *Pets-R-Permitted* (Annenberg Communications Institute, $9.95, Box 3930, Torrance, California 90510-3930) and *Take Your Pet USA* (Artco Publishing, $9.95, 12 Channel Street, Boston, Massachusetts 02210).

Start them young. Norton started traveling at six weeks. Smaller animals can often travel on their owners' laps or in the cabin. Don't fly them animal cargo if possible. Be sure the animal has had its shots and you've got papers to prove it. Check ahead: Hawaii and many nations have quarantine requirements. Check the useful booklet *Traveling with Your Pet* (send a $5 check to the ASPCA, 424 East 92nd Street, New York, New York 10128). "The best advice we can give for traveling with your pet," the ASPCA says, "is *don't* if you can possibly avoid it."

Don't Pets Need Universal Health Care Too?

"Wild Things" is loath to burden Bill and Hillary with yet another health-care crisis, but do they realize that fewer than one American pet in a hundred has health insurance? Sure, Socks, being First Cat, gets absolutely free, topflight medical care from army doctors. But 110 million ordinary cats and dogs are living with no coverage, exposing their owners to catastrophic medical expenses, such as $2,000 for a canine hip replacement, or a $100,000 bill for some very advanced dog cancer care or costly new pet dialysis treatments.

Given the priorities of many "Wild Things" readers, agonizing medical ethics choices such as, "Should we take our vacation in France, or should we let Lucky live?" are not choices at all. It's "Paris, maybe next year," they tell each other, huddled moist-eyed outside the recovery room, waiting for Lucky's vet to come out of the emergency room. For these true animal lovers, a major insurer, Fireman's Fund Insurance Company, has recently launched its nationwide Medipet pet insurance plan with the slogan "Because they're family too!" The $59-a-year Gold Tag plan buys you up to $3,000 coverage per illness, with a $300 deductible. If the pet is older than nine, the rate rises to $99 a year.

Armed with cable-TV infomercials aimed at twenty million viewers and a direct-mail campaign targeting another 600,000 households, Medipet is going to war with our nation's largest pet insurer, Veterinary Pet Insurance of Anaheim, California, which claims more than ninety thousand policies in thirty-seven states. Both insurers cover most medical treatments and hospitalization, but not preexisting conditions. Coverage is most helpful for catastrophic-illness care. (No pet hit by a car limps out of the ER these days for less than a grand.) But there are limits: Medipet refuses to pay for dog or cat psychiatry, root canals, or dental capping. VPI will not cover pets injured during war while "resisting attack" or during insurrection, rebellion, or revolution. Acupuncture, however, is covered. For more information, call Medipet at 1-800-528-4961 or VPI at 1-800-USA-PETS.

Dogs and cats are better risks than people, notes Michael Walters of the American Veterinary Medical Association. "They don't smoke, as a group. They rarely travel by automobile. And they are less likely to be victims of street crimes. So a lot of things that put people in the hospital don't put animals there."

Which Would You Rather Watch, a Video or Your Pet?

Americans spend $15 billion a year on movies and videos and $20 billion a year on their pets, according to *Time* magazine. This is why newspapers are a dying industry, since many still publish "Movies & Entertainment" sections but not entire "Pet" sections.

How Can I Enter My Pet in *Who's Who*?

Meet Irvine, California, resident Miss Alexandra O'Neil, who "never misses a meal. She eats baby food from a china plate. She thinks the turkey and lamb are just great. . . . She's a tiger-striped cat, four years old and a little fat." Do you wish the world to know of your shamelessly slavish love for your own adorable pet? Simply write to *Who's Who of Animals*, P.O. Box 2820, Durham, North Carolina 27715, and author John R. F. Breen will include your "biography of a great animal companion" for free. This is a red-bound, gold-embossed, $35 hardcover published recently by Companion Books, containing 1,200 biographies, including those of horses, rabbits, ferrets, a Wyoming moose (Ms. Mouse), an Iowa ladybug (Fred), and Garfield, who reveals his favorite foods to be "lasagna, Girl Scout cookies, and leg of mailman." Breen is now working on the second *Who's Who of Animals*.

How Can I Say I'm Sorry?

American Greetings, one of the world's largest greeting-card companies, has a new answer: the first line of pet greeting cards. With cuddly pet photos on the cover and paw prints padding across the envelopes, this new line of $1.65 cards congratulates new kitten births, mourns dog deaths, bids you happy birthday from a friend's pig, goldfish, or rabbit. Our favorite: the hind parts of a cat pictured with the legend YOU'RE NOBODY 'TIL YOU'VE BEEN IGNORED BY A CAT.

Who Does Consumer Testing for Dogs?

Meet Chops, senior test dog for *Good Dog! The Consumer Magazine for Dog Owners*, edited by Ross Becker of Charleston, South Carolina, who is listed as publisher of this national magazine, followed on the masthead by "Test Dogs: Chops, Flame, Max, and Jake" and "Feline Liaison: Jet Skicat."

"Chops is the senior test dog," says Becker. "She's been with the publication since the beginning, which was 1988. She's my dog, actually. She is in the office every day. And comes home with me at night."

Chops, a seventy-five-pound golden retriever–Bernese mountain dog mix, recently tested Pet Pupcorn, produced by the company that makes several other Chops favorites, such as Bowser Brittle (natural nut brittle made with whole-wheat flour, water, cashews, wheat germ, bran, and vanilla extract) and Bowownies, carob-flavored dog brownies. Chops *liked* Pet Pupcorn. She also liked the Forechewin Cookie, a fortune cookie for dogs made by Dandy Doggie in San Francisco. (Chop's fortune was "Dogwood is becoming to you.")

Chops's all-time favorites include Nookies Cookies ("Nookies Cookies are better than sex for dogs," says the Denver manufacturer), which produces the latest rage—vegetarian dog treats with real garlic and wheat flour. "The editors thought the vegetable Nookies Cookies were great with a little dab of cream cheese or pâté," Becker states.

Chops also likes Doggie Bagel Bites, small bagels for dogs, and *adores* a line of toys manufactured by Europet Toys in West Germany which features squeaky vinyl toys that resemble croissants and hoagie rolls. "She just loves her hoagie roll," Becker says.

Chops always gains a few pounds while doing consumer research for the "Doggie Treats" issue, then Becker pampers her with special diet food. "She's trimming her figure," he says.

Empire of Cats

We're happy to report that the remaining British Empire has fallen to cats. A poll of British cat lovers by *All About Cats* magazine found that 66 percent of male owners and 62 percent of female owners rated cats as more cuddly than their partners, according to the newspaper *Animal People*. Half of the cat lovers considered their cats better-looking, too.

What's the Most Pampered Cat in the United States?

The most pampered cat in our fine country is, according to *Time* magazine, Cherry Pop, a twelve-year-old Persian who rides in two miniature Rolls-Royces that match the Corniche of her owners, Florida socialites Vi and Huey Vanek. We're not making this up. At her last birthday party, at a posh oceanfront hotel in Fort Lauderdale, Cherry Pop was serenaded by a nine-piece orchestra that played her favorite tune, "Unforgettable." The Vaneks have already turned down $50,000 from a smitten Japanese investor who wanted to buy Cherry Pop, and Robin Leach is hot on the trail of Cherry Pop's story as well.

"Wild Things" is not impressed. We know all Americans pamper their pets *at least* as wildly as this. Send your "Impossibly Pampered Pet" stories to "Wild Things" at P.O. Box 63, Riverton, New Jersey 08077, with all the lavish details, and we will spend ten years working on a 1,000-page biography of your pet (or at least include him or her in our syndicated column one Thursday morning). Promise.

CHAPTER 8

AVOIDING BEASTLY THINGS

HOW *NOT* TO BE DEVOURED BY FLORIDA ALLIGATORS,
CALIFORNIA GREAT WHITE SHARKS,
AFRICAN KILLER BEES, NILE CROCODILES,
OR PENNSYLVANIA BLACK BEARS

Why Are Florida Alligator Attacks Increasing? How Can I Protect Myself?

This is truly heartwarming news: The Florida alligator has made a remarkable comeback from the brink of extinction!

Recently the "Wild Things" staff counted more than five hundred alligators on a visit to South Florida, many of them only inches from our pickup truck. "Go away!" our host shouted once, shooting a rubber band at one twelve-foot Goliath out the truck window. This failed to work.

True, we were in the actual Everglades, a large, gator-infested marsh, but the fact is there are now *one million* potentially man-eating alligators in Florida. This proves that (a) the Endangered Species Act works and should be strengthened by Congress; and (b) the youth of America are much more likely to be eaten by Florida alligators than their parents were.

Of course, the alligator doesn't *mean* to bite you. In all likelihood, you've been mistaken for a large bird, small dog, or rival alligator, and (after a bump and a bite on the head to determine your species, size, and strength) will be let go with a "YEEEEECH! Hey, sorry, it was an accident."

As Florida park ranger Paula J. Benshoff puts it, "The head of a swimming man is hard to distinguish from a raccoon or other animal . . . this [testing] bite is inconsequential to a full-grown alligator, but it can be quite hazardous to the human head."

Alligator attacks on humans, unheard of as recently as the 1970s in Florida, now number almost one hundred (most of them similiar to bad dog bites), with five confirmed deaths and four "unconfirmed" deaths. Why? Too many people settling or vacationing in Florida, invading the alligators' habitat. To avoid becoming an "accidental tourist," clip and save this "Wild Things" guide:

Don't walk your dog by a canal. One of Florida's most recent fatalities was a young girl walking along a canal with her dog, whose presence drew the gator out of the canal, whereupon he grabbed the girl.

Don't swim or run straight away. If you survive the alligator's first, astonishing burst of speed, you can win the footrace. Jog in a zigzag pattern and the alligator, incredibly, won't even see you—when it comes to peripheral vision, gators are no Larry Bird. In deep water, take a dive—alligators attack only on the surface and can't see well underwater. In shallow water, jump up and wave your arms wildly and yell. Remember: *Crawl* rhymes with *maul*.

Don't feed the alligators. Florida Statute 372.667 prohibits feeding all gators who are not University of Florida football players. This law was passed because of Marshall, a lumbering, much-loved alligator who lived on Sanibel Island with many rich retirees who used to feed him popcorn and bologna sandwiches and pat him on the head and say things like "You remind me of my son George, who's up north now." The wonderful thing about Marshall, aside from his friendly nature, was the more you fed him, the less you heard annoying dog-barking in Sanibel.

Marshall lived to a ripe old age but finally died, leading to much civic mourning and even calls for an autopsy. Alas, countless undigested dog collars were found in Marshall's stomach, whereupon State Law 372.667 was rushed through the Florida legislature. This was the origin of the "Marshall Plan."

How Dangerous Are Spider Bites?

Relax, arachnophobes. There's nothing to worry about. Oh, sure, there *was* that California woman who was vacuuming her carpet in 1993 when she felt a tingling bite on her thigh, a tiny nibble from the common reclusive brown spider. The next thing she knew, she was waking up in a hospital bed without her arms, legs, or nose, all of which had to be amputated to save her life from blood poisoning. But this was an almost unheard-of allergic reaction.

You're much more likely to die from a lightning strike or a skiing accident than from a spider bite, says a University of California entomologist. In an average year, forty-three Americans die from insect bites—about half from allergic reactions to honeybee stings.

What Are My Odds of Being Killed by a Grizzly Bear?

For each person killed by a black bear, seventeen people have died from spider bites, twenty-five from snakebites, sixty-seven from domestic-dog attacks, and ninety thousand have been murdered by human beings. Grizzlies are twice as deadly as the black bear. You figure the math.

How to Avoid Great White Sharks

Recently the "Wild Things" staff went to the beach, which gave us a warm, nostalgic feeling inside. Like many Americans, we have not been to the beach since 1975, when the movie *Jaws* was released.

Jaws, as most of you know, was a shark slasher flick with a *fake machine monster*. Nonetheless, it has ruined the human experience with most of the planet (i.e., the oceans) for almost two decades now.

In honor of summer, "Wild Things" decided to investigate the truth about how to avoid great white shark attacks so Americans can put their *Jaws* fears behind them once and for all.

Why to Be Afraid. By studying photos of actual great white sharks going "Aaahhh," you will realize that *Jaws* was probably a public service. Great whites are, in fact, the largest predators on earth, with a preference for large, warm-blooded prey (such as people). Yes, Moby Dick fans, the sperm whale is the largest big-prey predator that has ever lived (twice again as big as the realistic T. rex in *Jurassic Park*). But Moby Dick feeds on squid and other large cold-blooded creatures, and we have nothing to fear from it. And yes, the killer whale (remember *Free Willy*?), at thirty-three feet and ten tons, is a savage predator that can snap up a great white shark in a few bites, but it has never attacked humans in the wild.

Why Not to Be Afraid. Great whites have made more than one hundred documented attacks on humans worldwide since 1950, twenty-two of them fatal. Heck, twenty-two people die every day in the United States from *bee stings*. About twenty-five people a year die from shark attacks, but great whites are responsible for only about 12 percent of shark attacks on humans. Great-white attacks receive more publicity because of (a) *Jaws*, the book and the movie; and (b) the great white shark, like the American pit bull terrier, causes the most spectacular damage of its species due to the awesomely destructive first bite.

Avoid the Red Triangle. More than half of all documented white-shark attacks have occurred along the 120-mile coastline between Monterey Bay and Tomales Point, centering on San Francisco—the Great White Shark Attack Capital of the World. (Most of the world's shark experts and trackers live near this Red Triangle, so the reporting is higher.) Great whites show a preference for surfers, who look like seals from below—most notably Lewis Boren, who on December 19, 1981, had his torso removed by a twenty-foot great white that bit clear through the surfboard. Florida is the other domestic beach to be wary of: fourteen shark attacks in '81, for instance, and two deaths.

Avoid Southern Australia. This is notorious great-white snacking country, and the presence of British-style tabloids means your relatives will have to read headlines like SHARK

RIPS WOMAN IN TWO. This happened in 1985 to Shirley Ann Durdin, thirty-three, mother of four, who was snorkeling in shallow Peake Bay when a twenty-foot great white bit her in half. South Africa is the other foreign beach to avoid; Peter Gimbel filmed *Blue Water, White Death* there.

Don't Use Head & Shoulders. In his 1990 paper on the history of shark repellents, "Shark Repellent: Not Yet, Maybe Never," U.S. Navy shark expert H. David Baldridge concluded that shampoo and dishwashing liquid do not work as shark repellents.

"Single White Pointer" Needs Home. The "white pointer" is an informal name for "great white shark" which shows you are an *experienced marine biologist*. This is certainly the greatest euphemism in all of nature. (Parent Number One: "Honey, what should we get the kids for Christmas? A blue-point Himalayan cat, a German shorthaired pointer, or a white pointer?" Parent Number Two: "Better go for the white pointer. Buffy's allergic to cats, and it says here in *The Purebred Puppy Buyer's Guide* that the German shorthair can be 'noisy, restless, and prone to destructive chewing.' "

How Dangerous Are Killer Bees, Really?

In Venezuela, between 1975 and 1988, about 350 people were killed by killer bees—or about 2.1 deaths per million people. This is about as common as death by snakebites, lightning strikes, or malaria—i.e., not common at all.

Mark L. Winston, author of *Killer Bees: The Africanized Honey Bee in the Americas*, says the media has overhyped the Africanized-bee invasion in our hemisphere ever since *Time* magazine coined the headline KILLER BEES in 1965.

But "Wild Things" believes if a new animal was discovered in our neighborhood as deadly as lightning or snakes, it would be an alarming development indeed. (GIANT TOAD SWALLOWS MAILMAN. NOT TO WORRY, EXPERTS SAY; IT HAPPENED ONLY 350 TIMES IN THE NINETIES.)

We recommend that you not settle in the southern third of the United States, where these monsters are headed. Unless, of course, you get a high-paying job with a company car and can afford a house in a neighborhood with good schools.

How Dangerous Are Honeybees?

In the United States, about twenty people a year die from honeybee stings, a rate of about 0.08 deaths per year per million people.

Killer Crocs!

As children we were all glad to hear that the United States is a very powerful country, which since 1776 has enjoyed the vast advantage of having an ocean separating it from Europeans and other warlike creatures, namely, the African crocodile. Unfortunately we must report this is no longer true. Just when you thought it was safe to go back in the water, some yahoos, who will no doubt be swallowed whole for their greed, have imported *Crocodylus niloticus* to our hemisphere to make Nile-crocodile pocketbooks. And the crocs, experts says, are headed our way.

"Big deal," you say. Consider: The Nile croc is a twenty-foot, one-ton monster that has devoured more humans than any other African creature for centuries and has not done any sensitivity training or volunteer charity work in 100 million years, i.e., in the Cretaceous Period. If this sounds like *Jurassic Park*, you get the idea. Nile crocs are almost twice the size of Florida alligators, ten times as mean, and eat humans on purpose, not by accident.

This brings us to today's monster-animal-in-the-news grammar question: When this classic African man-eater starts devouring Florida residents of both sexes, will newspapers report it as the MAN-EATING CROCODILE or PERSON-EATING CROCODILE? This is the kind of distinction that really matters to journalists, and we recommend the nation's newspaper editors adopt a nonsexist crocodile headline style to correct a centuries-old injustice, since most of the croc's victims have been washerwomen along the Nile.

So when you see the headline PERSON-EATING CROC DOWNS LOCAL MAN on the back page of the sports section, above all, *don't panic*. We journalists now specialize in public service, so here are three reasons not to worry that the most fearsome person-eater in history is now in our hemisphere.

1. *Brazil is a long way away.* Ecologists worldwide sent protest faxes and telexes when Brazilian authorities approved the crocodile-breeding farm in Osório, six hundred miles south of Rio, but this is thousands of miles from New York City. When the African killer bees started out in these parts, it took them thirty-three years to reach Texas. Crocs will have to make the trip on their bellies. So we have time.

2. *The crocs are locked up.* The annual output of 4,800 baby crocs are kept from freedom by *two* concrete walls, a steel door, and a boxer dog named Panther, who has introduced the whole notion of canine psychiatry to South America. "Escape is next to impossible," owner Andreia

Fillippi says, the exact words used by the guy who imported a couple of African bees to Brazil in '56. "They will get out," says a croc specialist. "They will eat many people. They will change the way the West relates to water."

3. *We won't have to worry about alligators anymore.* The African crocs will take care of this problem by driving the gator to near extinction, some experts say. "If you're standing by a canal, you're fair game," says Richard Farinato, a wildlife specialist with the Humane Society of the United States. "This is a very, very impressive animal, and none of those at American zoos are nearly as big as they get in the wild. They're just too big [and dangerous] to keep in zoos."

What Should I Do When a Gorilla Charges?

We'll be perfectly frank: We much prefer vacations where the central question is "Where should we visit first, France or Italy?"

But with ecotourism all the rage, "Wild Things" realizes that more vacationing Americans are asking what it means when the six-hundred-pound male silverback bares his teeth, beats his chest, and charges.

Worry not: The big guy's just bluffing.

Gorillas are generally shy, relatively gentle vegetarians, "not at all interested in snatching humans, climbing towers, or swatting planes from the sky," says Janine M. Benyus, author of *Beastly Behaviors*.

When the silverback charges, just *don't move.* "This is very hard to do," allows naturalist Will Weber of Ann Arbor, Michigan, who leads five-hour hikes into the Rwandan rain forest to within handshake distance of Dian Fossey's *Gorillas in the Mist*. "But it works every time."

What's the World's Deadliest Snake?

The African death adder *sounds* to us like the deadliest
snake, but the harmless-sounding Australian small scale
snake is the prince of poison in all of nature. One bite is
enough to kill instantly 250,000 mice. This is enough poison to cause human death in approximately the amount of
time it takes to say, "Small scale snake? Whew. At least it's
not an African dea—"

A Safe Wilderness Experience: Dumpster Bears

Recently the "Wild Things" staff ventured into Pennsylvania's Pocono Mountains, where we witnessed two timeless
rites of spring: honeymooners in heart-shaped Jacuzzis
built into mirrored walls and wild black bears.

Our first morning in the rustic cabin by the lake, we
awakened to an awful *thump, ba-dump, barrroooar.* Yes,
we'd avoided the tacky hotels with red-velvet wallpaper to
commune with nature, and here was a visitor: a giant,
hungry black bear. I stayed inside to think about the
broader implications while my wife, mother-in-law, and
two-year-old daughter, Grace, rushed outside to take
pictures.

Bears are the most feared animal in North America. According to University of Calgary biology professor Stephen
Herrero, author of *Bear Attacks*, black bears have killed
twenty-four humans in the past century. The Bible is no
bear PR manual, either. "I will fall upon them like a bear
robbed of her cubs," Hosea wrote in the Old Testament. "I
will tear open their [*editor's note:* human] breast." This fear

is reinforced by the frequent terrifying encounters Americans have with bears in (a) Disney movies for children, and (b) the waiting areas of restaurants, where large stuffed black bears ferociously guard the toothpicks and mints.

A few minutes later, Grace came back smiling. The beast in the Dumpster was a very *nice* bear, she said. Grace had made a remarkable discovery: An excellent, affordable, and generally safe place to watch bears in their natural habitat is climbing around inside a Dumpster. Sure, for five grand a week you can journey to gorgeous Kodiak Island in the Gulf of Alaska and watch brown bears scoop salmon in one of the last remaining wild places free of human interferences (Irony Alert). However, if too many spectators show up on Kodiak Island, biologists believe, eventually the bears may change their diet to include spectators and PBS producers.

The fact is, death by black bear is extremely rare, according to Jeff Fair, wildlife biologist and author of *The Great American Bear*. Black bears do attack humans scores of times a year, inflicting mostly minor injuries. Most of these attacks, like bad marriages among humans, are the result of poor communication between species. Here's how to communicate with the most common bear in the northeastern United States, the Dumpster bear.

Never Pet a Bear and Say, "Good Doggie"

It's okay to get up close and watch or photograph the black bear without, of course, crowding it or petting it. Bears and people have mingled safely at dozens of garbage dumps for decades without serious injury, Fair says. But keep in mind: Wild bears hate to be petted. It violates their sense of the divide between species. Black bears nip or cuff bad-mannered people who crowd around or try to pet them at campsites, Fair says, but these injuries aren't serious.

Don't Worry if the Bear Charges

The most common black-bear attack is a terrifying, ferocious charge, wherein the beast roars straight at you like a hairy, triple-wide Dick Butkus and . . . deliberately misses the tackle! This is why there are so many good narrow-escape bear stories. Bears are almost always *just kidding*, trying to scare you away. Bears practice what evolutionary theorists call *restraint*—they've learned over the eons that conflict with a *potentially stronger species* doesn't pay.

Don't Back Down

Stand your ground during the charge. *Never run away from a black bear.* This, Fair says, may trigger *carnivore chase behavior.* Any form of mild human aggression tends to frighten away even a dominant bear. Stand up to a black bear, talk to him. If you fall and the bear sniffs you, *Play dead*.

If Your Luck Runs Out . . .

The above methods will fail tragically in the rarer form of bear attack known as *predaceous*. The black bear is a stealthy stalker and attacks from behind, Fair says, with a "quick, quiet, and clean debilitating attack directed toward the victim's head and neck, after which the bear carries its victim away." Don't let this happen to you.

This is the one-in-a-million bear who, possibly because he has escaped from Bellevue, stalks you like prey. In this case, Fair advises, "Never, never, never play dead." Strike the bear's nose, he says, with any weapon you can find. "Survivors of these attacks have driven the bears away using boots, rocks, an ax, canoe paddles, branches, and their own fists."

CHAPTER 9

BUGS & BARNYARD THINGS

HOW TO OUTWIT THE FLEA, EXPLOITED GROUNDHOGS,
MINDLESS ANTS, HIGH-IQ PIGS, CHICKENS WHO LISTEN
TO VIVALDI, AND DOOMED TURKEYS

If Fleas Have Survived 200 Million Years, How Can I Possibly Eradicate Them in a Few Days?

You can't. Today's flea is a superbug compared to those wimpy ancestors that wiped out a quarter of the population of Europe in the Black Death.

"Fleas have become resistant to practically everything safe to put on an animal," says University of Illinois entomologist Robert Metcalf. "They're almost impossible to kill." It's time to raise the white flag. Four decades of trying to find the perfect poison just hasn't worked. The flea has an incredible ability to mutate. It takes chemists years and at least $50 million to develop a new flea spray. And in two years the buggers simply scramble their genetics and are throwing keg parties with empty cans of Raid.

Despite the nonsense emanating from Madison Avenue, fleas, like love handles, are here to stay. Here's how to wage war and settle for a truce with the bloodthirsty suckers:

Vacuum bits of dried blood. The most awesome fact I have learned as a pet and animal journalist, aside from the number of times lions have sex in a day (this book is for the entire family, so we can't reveal the exact daily number except to say it's 155 times in fifty-five hours), is that your living-room carpet is splattered with microscopic bits of dried blood which are being used to breed creatures that killed more people than all the wars ever fought. The best nonchemical way to kill fleas is to vacuum daily with a strong vacuum cleaner. A flea (Awe Alert) can go eight months between meals (a little bite of blood from you or your cat or dog), meanwhile leaving fecal droppings on your carpet and furniture that flea larvae hungrily gobble up. Fleas love sand or pet hairs to help make their eggs, says University of Florida biologist Diana Simon, so Electrolux this all up. And change your vacuum bag frequently. Fleas Houdini out of vacuum bags all the time.

Nuke 'em. Flea dips and chemicals can be effective, but consult your vet for the safest ones. Many animals have had severe reactions to flea collars and get fleas anyway. (The flea repellent Blockade, which contains DEET, was recalled by Hartz Mountain in 1988 after more than one thousand pet poisonings or deaths were reported in Texas and Illinois. Blockade was reformulated before returning to the market.)

The National Coalition Against the Misuse of Pesticides (701 East Street SE, Suite 200, Washington, D.C.;

(202) 543-5450) recommends an insecticidal fatty-acid soap, such as Safer's Flea Soap for Dogs & Cats, and shampoos or sprays containing the citrus oil limonene. Diatomaceous earth, relatively harmless to people, can kill fleas if sprinkled sparingly into rugs and upholstery. For relatively harmless-to-humans toxins, the coalition recommends (as a last resort) pyrethrins, derived from the chrysanthemum plant, or methoprene, which prevents fleas from developing.

Be alert at all times. Following directions religiously would avoid many pet poisonings, say officials of the University of Illinois's animal poison control center. "Some people think, 'My cat has a real flea problem, I'd better double the dose,' " one official said.

Squish 'em. Some experts say crushing fleas with your fingernails may release disease organisms and isn't a good idea. But flea-combing them into a soapy cocktail is a safe technique. We say, whatever floats your flea. "Squash them between your fingernails or drown them or torture them," Dr. Karen Overall says. "Enjoy it," she advises. "It's one of your few clear victories in the unwinnable war."

How Has Groundhog Day, Like Christmas, Lost Its Spiritual Meaning?

Every February 2 marks our most important animal holiday, which is of course Groundhog Day. I have a confession: I love Groundhog Day. I loved it even before I started to dream about spending the same night over and over with Andie MacDowell, which happened after I watched Bill Murray perform this enviable trick in the great film *Groundhog Day*. I love it even though right now in my backyard thirty-six fat groundhogs are quietly hibernating under thirty-six narrow, snowswept knolls that crippled my lawnmower, waiting for spring. "Spring" is what we quaintly imagine they are waiting for, but on their calendars they have it marked as *Phase Three of tunnel extension project, side yard,* which they plan to complete before seeking state money for Phase Four, which involves uprooting my house.

Being a highly objective service column, "Wild Things" will (a) tell you how to more deeply appreciate Groundhog Day as one of the most significant times for the human spirit (we're not joking); (b) show you how Groundhog Day has lost its true meaning as our connection to the animal world, as Christmas has lost its meaning as our link to the divine, in a tide of commercialism and entertainment; and (c) provide tips on how to humanely nuke the darn woodchucks, the true rodent name for groundhog, in your backyard if they're bothering you, because, hey, you can't get the lawnmower over the mounds.

But first, this special note to readers in southern Florida and northern California: If you have any Spanish, German, French, Scottish, or other northern ancestry, February 2 affects you somewhere deep inside as the midpoint between bitter winter and sweet spring, even though you now live in the glorious Sun Belt and this makes little apparent sense. February 2 is halfway between the winter solstice and the spring equinox, the day our ancestors celebrated in folk culture as the one to turn our backs on winter and hope for spring. According to sociobiologists, your family could breed exclusively in the Sun Belt for tens of millions of years and you would still feel the timeless pull of hope on Groundhog Day.

Anyway, Groundhog Day the holiday, for those of you who've lost track, is an ancient village tradition wherein

America awaits for Punxsutawney Phil to emerge from his natural environment of an electrically heated den and search for his shadow between the glare of television lights and the long shadows cast by Punxsutawney Phil T-shirt stands.

According to tradition, if the groundhog comes out of his hole and sees his shadow in the Pennsylvania town of seven thousand folks, he'll hole up for six more weeks of winter; if he doesn't see his shadow, spring will come early. "He's right about 90 percent of the time," says Jimmy Means of the Punxsutawney Groundhog Club's Inner Circle. "It's just instinct." Well, almost. The result is actually decided in advance by the Inner Circle's fourteen members, who don tuxedos and top hats for the event. Ha! Ha! This is called "postmodern"—taking something old, and real, and recasting it for the evening news.

(There are actually more than a dozen Groundhog Day groundhogs in our fine country, but Jimmy from Sun Prairie, Wisconsin, has the biggest grievance for being left out of many national news stories because Sun Prairie has been cooking up its media event only since 1948. Punxsutawney has the advantage of having started its Groundhog Day in 1898 and Phil pops out of his hole an hour earlier than Jimmy for Eastern media deadlines.)

Thousands of years ago, before Eastern media deadlines and Accu-Weather, rural folk depended on what they called *folklore* to predict seasonal changes. They spied on hibernating bears, badgers, and woodchucks for signs of spring. It was life or death for farmers, that hope for the sun. The Christian church adopted the celebration as its Candlemas.

"If Candlemas Day be fair and clear, there'll be twa [two] winters in the year" was the chant of Scottish farmers. In France, Spain, and Germany, folks also invented the hopeful fiction that a groundhog who couldn't see his shadow (very likely on a cloudy winter day) would bring an early spring.

Tail end: To keep woodchucks from burrowing into your garden, bury your garden fence twelve inches below-ground, says Bill Adler, Jr., in *Outwitting Critters*. Drop dog droppings or a rag soaked in peanut or olive oil down the tunnel opening to stink the woodchucks out. Nasty gas cartridges, neutron bombs to woodchucks, are available at farm supply stores and from the U.S. Fish and Wildlife Service. If you use traps, wait until early summer, when your Punxsutawney Phil is well fed and can endure being released (i.e., abandoned) by you somewhere else. Ethel Hancock, who lives on a farm near Dongola, Illinois, recommends frying young groundhogs after putting them in a pressure cooker about five minutes and then seasoning them with salt and pepper and rolling them in flour. "They taste quite a bit like chicken to me," she says.

How Can I Feed the Birds Without Being Attacked?

At last, the sun beckons! Pitchers and catchers report to Florida, the cry of "Play ball!" is heard across the land, and 82.5 million Americans prepare for the blissful enjoyment of the nation's second most popular outdoor sport, which is, of course, bird feeding. This is a wonderful way to teach children about nature: beautiful birds migrate thousands of miles to our backyard, build nests, raise their young, and aim at our heads like squadrons of F-15 fighter planes. Yes, it's a moral imperative that we feed and help build nests for birds this time of year since we've polluted many of their habitats. But remember:

Bird feeding can be dangerous. In 1986 a nesting cardinal in Kansas City, Missouri, became the first known bird to force a postman to change routes. "He just kept dive-bombing the carrier's head," a postal source told us. "Never bothered the weekend carrier, he just hated that one post-man!" Possibly, our sources tell us, because he was just too tall! Mockingbirds, too, are notorious dive-bombers. "They make strafing runs at your head and sometimes give glanc-ing blows to the cranium or shoulder area," says Craig Tufts of the National Wildlife Federation. If you're lucky enough to have a bird nest in your front yard, Tufts ad-vises, just don't use the front door for three months. "After all," he says, "attacking birds are just being good parents."

Don't let children touch the nest. Repeated touching will leave a human "scent trail" for raccoons, who will waddle over expecting the usual Weight Watchers freezer cartons and wind up feasting on eggs. Mama bird won't mind if you take the kids over to visit the nest once every two weeks to peek at the eggs and, if you're incredibly lucky, see the babies leave the nest. Check the skies for Red Bar-ons first.

Feather the nest. Almost fifty kinds of birds, such as screech owls, chickadees, bluebirds, wrens, and purple mar-tins, can nest only in hollow trees or boxes. And now's the time to build or buy a "nest box," or birdhouse, to attract them—feathered, if you wish, with bits of string, yarn, or straw. Robins need mud to build their nests. "A five-year-old with a hose is very good at creating a mud puddle in your yard," Tufts says. Build it, and they will come.

Fill the gap. The dried apple husks and seed in farmers'

fields that fed birds in the winter are gone, and spring has yet to provide its bounty. So birds will welcome a between-seasons snack at the feeder now. "And if you keep it up into the summer," says Sue Wells of the National Bird Feeding Society in Northbrook, Illinois, "you can watch them take teach their babies to eat out of your feeder. It's a fantastic hobby and, unlike skiing, it doesn't take any skill!"

Flea Facts

The flea is remarkably adapted to suck blood. Consider, for instance, the cat flea. Magnified thousands of times, the cat flea looks like a lobster! Spindly legs with backward-pointing bristles, ideal for combing through cat and dog hairs to reach soft skin. A head that is mostly beak for piercing skin, mouth parts perfect for slurping, and, most impressive, disproportionately huge hind legs for leaping. The cat flea slowly winds up these incredible exploding elastic protein pads that it calls feet and—*Boom!*—"fires" into the air—as far as eight inches high and thirteen inches across—catapulting onto your cat, dog, or you. If we had equal ability, proportionately we could jump one thousand feet straight up.

Why Does the Bible Say, "Go to the Ant, Thou Sluggard; Consider Her Ways, and Be Wise?"

Several readers have asked if ants possess some secret of a wise social order that humans can learn from. So I turned to the world's leading myrmecologist (ant expert), E. O.

Wilson of Harvard University, who says the biblical proverb expresses an admiration for industrious ants, which scientists share. Ants are among the world's most highly organized and altruistic critters, Wilson says, who routinely sacrifice their lives for the commonweal. Would humans be wise to "consider her ways"? "God, I hope not," Wilson told me. Millions of ants in colonies act as a simple organism, mindlessly following chemical trails. "Ants have no free will, and free will, in the end, is what gives mankind its capacity to destroy but also its genius, its cause for hope," Wilson said. Consider E.O.'s ways, and be wise.

How Do Farm Animals Rank in Intelligence?

The pig is the Einstein of farm animals. Pigs are at least as intelligent as dogs and rival the brainpower of dolphins and chimpanzees. The brilliance of pigs was made plain to "Wild Things" when we visited a farm with our three-year-old daughter and a big sign on the pig pen warned: PIGS BITE. DO NOT FEED. The cows, sheep, and goats were happy to be stroked and fed bits of corn, but the pigs were too angry brooding about the waste of their vast intelligence.

This is literally true. "Pigs are so smart that when they're cooped up in a small space they get very frustrated that they cannot properly express their intelligence," said Melanie Adcock, farm-animals director of the Humane Society of the United States, which celebrates National Farm Animal Awareness Week the third week in September, with bus and subway signs in Denver, Colorado, and Columbus, Ohio.

The Humane Society is best known as a champion of cats and dogs, but it is honoring cows, pigs, and chickens this week of the year because most Americans mistake them for the three food groups, hamburgers, hot dogs, and chicken Dijonaise. Adcock hopes that "greater awareness of the intelligence and sensitivity of farm animals will lead to better treatment." Many Americans would argue that barbecue is a better treatment than Dijonaise, but to these Americans Adcock issues a warning: Science has recently discovered that chickens can recognize one hundred other chickens on sight by facial features and can learn up to fifty words, the worst of which, we imagine, are reserved for the fleshy creature in the Happy Hen BBQ apron.

Consider also:

Chickens prefer classical music. Chickens apparently rank second in farm-animal intelligence, as evidenced by their favorite composer, who is Vivaldi. This was discovered by a farmer who noticed that chickens were clucking happily in the henhouse when he played a classical music tape. Upon hearing Vivaldi, the chickens clucked *and* blissfully followed the farmer around. Chickens much preferred the "Spring" movement to "Winter."

Elvis tops cow charts. One herd studied by scientists produced more milk while listening to the King. This was supported by another study that showed that cows generally prefer rock 'n' roll to other music. "Imagine being a classical-music cow," Adcock says, "in a rock herd. It would be horrible."

Pigs prefer southern exposure. Pigs are very smart diggers. "Pigs like to dig up earth, check everything out," Adcock says. "Some farmers use them to turn over a whole field, they're so good at it." There are guard pigs, truffle-sniffing pigs, and pigs who outsmart dogs in American Kennel Club training exercises. Left to themselves, an extended family of pigs will build an elaborate nest of leaves and twigs, using a sophisticated division of labor. The pigs build their nests always facing south, presumably for the superior light needed for painting, and up on a hill, to be closer to God.

Why Would Anyone Want a Miniature Pet Cow?

Miniature animals, such as thirty-six-inch-high cows and tiny cattle, horses, sheep, and donkeys, are popular for the same reason ferrets are a hit, birds are all the rage, and cats became the national pet, says Purdue University animal expert Alan Beck. Working moms, single parents, latchkey kids, and most others want a low-maintenance pet. Beware, cautious Maureen Neidhardt, editor of *Rare Breeds Journal*. Trendy pets are almost always more trouble than they're worth. Minihorses, for example, can be messy, and can cost $5,000 for a filly and $15,000 for a stallion. With a little research, you can find a homeless pet pig, snake, or parrot—previously "in" pets that went "out" of a lot of houses—for cheap.

Flea Facts

Leaping fleas accelerate fifty times faster than the space shuttle, according to Defend Flea and Tick Products.

How Many Turkeys Give Their Lives for Thanksgiving?

For many years we celebrated Thanksgiving in Massachusetts, not far from where the Pilgrims landed. And still today our family gathers in New England, in a big old house filled with warm aromas and the long shadows of candle-light, to give thanks for the amazingly low IQ of the turkey that has once again accepted our invitation to dinner. Yes, gobbler SAT scores have been a national concern ever since a flock of the birds managed to drown in the rain in a parade in Texas by staring at the sky, whereupon thousands of patriotic Americans gave thanks that the Founding Fathers wisely ignored Ben Franklin's suggestion that the turkey be the national bird. This is a true story.

But the "Wild Things" staff has learned the highest philosophical justification for eating turkey on Thanksgiving is not their stupidity or succulence but the horrible alternative. Yes, we're referring to the year we accepted the invitation of our friend Sandi, an extremely talented radical feminist and vegetarian poet, to dine on tofu turkey. This caused "Wild Things" to make a lifetime vow never to be strictly vegetarian, yet we sympathize with those who are trying to raise the world's humane consciousness, just as we are not Hindu but admire the teachings of Gandhi. So herewith, a guide to a more humane holiday:

Consider Linda McCartney's tofu turkey. Paul's famous vegetarian wife calls it a "Festive Sunday Roast with Savory Stuffing," but the main ingredient, as far as we can determine, is "5 Veggie Tofu–brand burgers processed in food processor with ¾ cup water." Yum! The flavor is enhanced by "1½ tbsp water mixed with 1½ tsp egg replacer," and "¼ cup textured vegetable protein (TVP)." Preheat oven to 350 degrees Fahrenheit and begin speed-dialing friends and neighbors to see if they have an extra place at *their* table.

If this, however, truly appeals to you, call the People for Ethical Treatment of Animals' tofu-turkey hotline at (301) 770–7433. You'll hear Mr. Subliminal, as played by "Saturday Night Live" comedian Kevin Nealon, tell you how to receive free veggie Thanksgiving recipe cards, including cashew gravy and the McCartney roast. We're not fabricating any of this.

Consider the carnage. From the turkey perspective, our cherished national holiday is Black Thursday. Forty million turkeys will end up stuffed the week before Thanksgiving, joining 200 million that go to the gallows the rest of the year, said Tracy Reiman, PETA's international vegetarian-campaign coordinator. Wild turkeys run 55 mph and live twelve years; turkeys raised to be stuffed can barely lift their hormone-injected heads and live twenty weeks. PETA has spared the lives of four of these turkeys, Dominic, Eugene, Sammy, and Freddy, who are invited as "guests of honor, not the main course," to PETA's annual Thanksgiving dinner each year, which differs from the original Pilgrim feast only in that four live turkeys sit in their own seats pecking corn.

Relax: Corn doesn't have feelings. This is not something that troubled Captain John Smith, but it has lately been discussed in our society. "Every now and then somebody will say, 'Oh, vegetables have feelings too,' " Reiman said. "But we know that vegetables do not have nervous systems like animals and do not try to get away or resist and, we believe, do not experience pain. This is an absurd statement usually made by somebody who knows they're doing wrong by eating turkey and tries to blame us for eating corn."

Consider humane gobblers. According to the Humane Society of the United States, most turkeys sold in supermarkets are raised en masse in huge, overcrowded, barren, climate-controlled buildings filled with fumes and dust that cause frequent turkey heart attacks. In health food stores, co-ops, specialty markets, and some supermarkets you can find more humanely raised turkeys, which will be labeled "organic," "free-range," "free-running," "free-roaming." PETA says these "free-range" turkeys also live short, miserable lives. The only worse fate than hearing Bob Woodward on the other end of the phone say, "I'm investigating your private life" is to be subject to a PETA protest, which the Iowa Turkey Federation learned on December 1, 1993. A giant costumed turkey did impressive symbolic things under the banner TURKEYS GIVE THANKS FOR VEGETARIANS.

Will Bugs Outlast the Human Race?

When deep, sweet July is upon us, folks dream of baseball, beaches, and long vacations, denying the essential truths of summer: (a) According to the *New York Times*, there are three hundred pounds of bugs for every pound of human being. (b) Wherever you go, you are always near a bug. When your plane is landing at the airport, undiscovered species of beetles are in the grass by the runway, quietly humming—with satisfaction, no doubt, since 25 percent of all known species of living things (350,000 different species) are beetles. (c) Beetles will be scuttling through the ruins of our cities long after humankind perishes.

This is something people love to repeat, but is it true? To find out, we called Sue Hubbell, author of the delightful summer companion *Broadsides from the Other Orders: A Book of Bugs*. Hubbell is right now traveling the nation with a cage of pet camel crickets that she observes having sex at night under infrared light. This puts her in the minority of Americans, most of whom never watch camel crickets having sex and who, to judge from a recent national survey, have no desire to witness the Joy of Bugs. (According to social scientists at the University of Arizona, only 0.7 percent of Americans actually *like* bugs, 90 percent said they *hated* bugs or were terrified of them, and the rest tolerated them.)

The answer, Hubbell says, is "Who knows?" But bet on the bugs. The silverfish, for instance, a bug that lives off the glue in the binding of paperback copies of *Jurassic Park*, crawled wormlike out of the primeval sea *long* before the dinosaurs (when humans were, best we can tell, embarrassing emissions of ocean-vent gas). Silverfish, Hubbell says, "would regard humans tenderly . . . as a young, trial species . . . [who] will very likely disappear in the next mass extinction."

Bugs will outlast us because:

Bugs have great sex. Silverfish enjoy a tail-wagging love dance that the German entomologist Von H. Sturm lovingly described in 1915 in his paper "Die Paarung beim Silberfischen." Male Parnassius butterflies secrete a fluid that seals up the female's reproductive opening; if the male holds on too long, it's "coitus perpetuus," Hubbell says. Dragonflies use 80 percent of their brains to run those huge eyes, but still can't see so well: They try to mate with shadows and, sometimes, birds. What makes bug sex successful in the long term is simple: vast numbers of offspring.

Bugs don't use air conditioners. Humans are a fussy, fragile species. "If it gets too hot, we need to make ourselves cool through technology. If it gets too cold, we need coats or we can freeze to death." Most bugs aren't affected at all by temperature. Environmental "crises" are usually just changes in the earth's chemistry that are "crises for *us*," Hubbell says. Lots of bugs will probably thrive under those holes in the ozone layer.

We're wasting our money on bugs. Better we fix the ozone layer or the deficit. Americans spend $3.5 billion a year killing bugs, which "must make us feel safe," Hubbell says sarcastically, but is often "completely ludicrous." Most bugs don't hurt or help us.

Flea Facts

A female flea drinks fifteen times her body weight in blood daily and lays a couple thousand eggs.

How Did Three-Hundred-Pound Pigs Become Popular Household Pets?

It's time for our new feature, "Monster Animals in the News." This timely and important story, no doubt occurring near you, concerns those tiny, adorable, high-IQ pot-bellied pigs from Vietnam maturing into ... nasty, slobbering, two-hundred-pound hogs that rip open refrigerator doors and chow down on everything but the Sears Coldspot.

We'll go on location to Minot, North Dakota, where the normally understated Associated Press reported this trend under the headline CUTE, EXOTIC PIG TURNS INTO 125-POUND MONSTER.

But first, a quote from an actual giant pig named Hog Along Cassidy as his owner, an actual Presbyterian minister in Austin, Texas, named Jim Rigby, tries to pick him up and put him in a kitty-litter box: "SQUEEEE! SQUEEE! EEEEEEEEEEEEEEEEEEEE!"

"Pigs squeal at 110 decibels," Nancy Cardillo, publisher of *Pot-Bellied Pigs* magazine, told us. "A jet engine is 105 decibels."

Next, Hog Along crushed a battery with his jaws. Tore the bathroom to pieces. Ripped up the living-room rug. And showed his alarmingly high pig IQ by emptying a bag of cedar shavings and carefully spreading them around the house to make a giant pig litter box. "He was a baby Godzilla," Rigby told the *Wall Street Journal.*

Whither the Perfect Novelty Pet of yesteryear? Surely you remember the Vietnamese pot-bellied pig, the trendy pet of the nineties—touted as no bigger than a cocker spaniel, smarter and more affectionate than a dog, poops in a cat litter box, can be taught to play "Twinkle, Twinkle, Little Star" on the piano . . .

Rigby, like twenty-five thousand other Americans, was promised a small (30–60-pound), loving pig, cleaner and smarter than a dog. Once folks paid $10,000 for such pigs. A New Orleans police pig sniffed for drugs! A St. Louis Super Pig named Peekee Wenthe saved a bank executive from a fire!

We knew the days of swine and roses were over when we saw the AP dispatch, slugged BRITE-FAT PIG, from North Dakota: "Frankie," short for Frankfurter, had grown from 5 pounds to 125 and looked like Jabba the Pig. When the nice Walsh family put their new pet on a diet, Frankie devoured six pounds of cat food before being caught. "Then he was sick for a week," said nice Jimmy Walsh, eleven. Then the Walshes found out Frankie's life span was twenty years!

Yes, in the great American tradition of lifting up and

tearing down, the ideal piglet of '91 has been getting some bad reviews lately for growing up . . . and up . . . and out. Homeless pet pigs have been spotted at dog pounds from Bucks County to the Main Line and, in one case, running loose in the Italian Market in South Philadelphia.

Many have sadly fulfilled the destiny of their cute names, such as Francis Bacon and Porkchop.

PEOPLE WHO WENT HOG-WILD FOR TINY PORKERS NOW RUE THE DAY "ORCA" MOVED IN, the *Wall Street Journal* intoned in 1993. Then *USA Today* jumped on the cart: PET PIGLETS BE-COMING A BOAR FOR SOME OWNERS. *Pot-Bellied Pigs* magazine, the respected national journal out of Ooltewah, Tennessee, struck back in its November issue: DON'T BOAR US WITH NEGA-TIVE JOURNALISM, JUST GIVE US A TIGHT "HOG."

The problem here: really bad puns. And irresponsible breeders. "People were breeding pot-bellies with [1,200-pound] farm sows," Cardillo says. Happily, the small, clean, loving pig is still the rule, she says. *Caveat emptor:* Make sure your house-pet piglet is at least six to eight weeks old, has all its shots, is registered with the Pot-Bellied Pig Registry Service (22819 Stanton Road, Lakeville, Indi-ana 46536) or the smaller International Gold Star Registry (Box 1478, Pacifica, California 94044). And for land's sake, meet the parents first. Or else, as they say in pig Latin, *Re-frigerator emptor.*

How Can I Save My Dogs and Cats from Pesticide Poisoning?

Spring is in the air, and so are potentially dangerous pesti-cides. Yes, it's time to make your lawn green and insect-free, that annual American passion that can make pets and people ill or dead. Herewith, a "Wild Things" *Safer Lawn Care Guide* in honor of Casey, the beloved Irish terrier of the late Philadelphia mayor Frank Rizzo. Casey died in 1981 after ingesting a pesticide that had been used on his grass by a major pesticide company, and Rizzo sued them and won a settlement out of court.

Dogs get cancer. The National Cancer Institute released a study last year that found a sixfold increase in lymphatic cancers in dogs whose owners frequently used lawn herbicides containing 2, 4-D, which is found in 1,500 pesticides and was a major component of Agent Orange. "Don't read the labels, just don't buy the damn stuff," says Dr. Michael Fox, president of the Humane Society of the United States. "These are highly toxic chemicals still on the market because the petrochemical-pharmaceutical-medical-agribusiness-industrial complex profits on harmful chemicals that make pets and people sick and then treats them to make them well. It's screwed up."

Pesticides harm cats. Powerful bug pesticides can be dangerous to all pets, says the American Animal Hospital Association. These chemical are organophosphates, and includes common pesticides such as Diazinon and malathion. "Cats are more sensitive to organophosphates than dogs," says Virginia veterinarian Peggy Rucker. Small, old, or young animals are most vulnerable. "Poisoning symptoms include difficulty breathing, excessive salivation, drooling, vomiting, runny eyes, diarrhea, seizures, and a coma," Rucker says. Keep pets away from sprayed areas for at least one day, and contact your vet if one or more symptoms appear. Christina Locek, Illinois concert pianist and champion ice-skater, testified to Congress in 1991 that insecticide spray from a neighbor's yard killed her cat and dog and left her legally blind and permanently disabled.

Representatives of the $1.5 billion lawn-care industry testified that their products were safe when used according to directions.

Use natural products. Natural, safe products can make beautiful lawns, Fox says. For more information, write to the National Coalition Against the Misuse of Pesticides, 530 Seventh Street SE, Washington, D.C. 20003; or Rodale Press, 33 East Minor Street, Emmaus, Pennsylvania 18049. The University of Illinois National Animal Poison Control Center, 1-800-548–2423, fields animal poison questions.

Call for help. But remember, if you call the National Animal Poison Control Center for advice on these matters, it doesn't come free. If you call the 800 number—a number used often in emergencies, often by vets—you'll pay $30 for a consultation. 1-900-680–0000, at $2.95 a minute, offers the same service. If your pet has been poisoned by a product made by a major manufacturer that has contracted with the help line, the center will give you free advice, says director William Buck.

Mosquito-Free Europe

Radio Fugue FM, a station fifty miles north of Paris, France, broadcasts (along with its regular fare) an ultrasound frequency at sixteen kilohertz, inaudible to humans but the same frequency as that emitted by male mosquitoes to keep the bloodsucking females away. A radius of four meters around the radio will be "free of biting mosquitoes," the station says.

Flea Facts

According to a recent scientific finding, a flea's armor is tougher than an M-1 tank.

CHAPTER 10

CHILDREN & BITING THINGS

DOG BITES, THE NUMBER-ONE KID HEALTH PROBLEM;

SECRET HOURS WHEN ZOO ANIMALS ARE *AWAKE*;

AND HOW TO SELECT GOLDFISH, TURTLES, ANT FARMS,

AND RETICULATED PYTHONS,

ONLY ONE OF WHICH CAN KILL YOU

Why Are So Many People Adopting Nice Family Pets, Like Giant, Potentially Fatal Snakes?

Yes, it's time to confront a disturbing trend in pet-owning America: The Age of Reptiles has returned. *Warning for human readers: According to top sociobiologists at Harvard University studying our innate fear of reptiles, the proper response to this piece is "Aaaiiiieeeee!"* Yes, according to the largest reptile census, taken in 1991, there are 735,000 pet snakes in this country, along with 708,000 turtles, 314,000 lizards, and 280,000 "other reptiles," some of whom may very well be middle managers in large industrial corporations. Snake and lizard pet ownership has doubled since 1987 (fortunately, to only 0.2 percent of households). Four-foot iguanas who walk on leashes and dine on scrambled eggs are the hottest cold-blooded pets. Geckos are all the rage in New York City, billed as nontoxic cockroach eliminators.

Reptiles "make real good pets for people on the go because they aren't demanding," one pet-store owner told us. "They don't smell, don't destroy your house, and don't make a sound." Yes, you can go away for a weekend and leave them for a few days and they won't miss you. You can feed your eighteen-foot python a pig and it won't need a meal until summertime. You can accidentally be swallowed whole by your pet python and it won't miss you. It's the perfect pet for the nineties: one with *no emotions at all*.

Certainly "Wild Things" believes we should teach our children that reptiles are not evil and deserve to live, but why a family would choose them over cats, dogs, and other human-bonded critters is a mystery to us. And would have been to Linnaeus, who once said, "Reptiles are abhorrent because of their cold body, pale color, cartilaginous skeleton, filthy skin, fierce aspect, calculating eye, offensive smell, harsh voice, squalid habitation and terrible venom."

"We don't recommend keeping reptiles as pets," says Rachel Lamb of the Humane Society of the United States. "They're not domesticated animals, they are more difficult than advertised to care for properly; there's no bond there, and there's even evidence reptiles may be psychologically damaged being kept as pets. Let's get homes for all the cats and dogs that need them first."

Recently we heard about a fifteen-year-old Colorado boy found strangled next to his giant pet snake. Fortunately pythons are responsible for only a very few deaths each year. "On a few occasions, a snake will attack," says Philip Samuelson, editor of *Reptiles & Amphibians* magazine. "Especially if a person smells of a food item that the snakes like. But most problems of that nature are avoidable."

Don't keep a snake that grows bigger than seven feet. If you're shopping in the twenty-foot python family, a Burmese python is a little mellower and therefore a better family pet than the reticulated python, although, as Samuelson once told us, "You certainly wouldn't want to leave it on the living-room rug with a newborn baby."

Why Should We Bother Saving the Rain Forests?

"Wild Things" offers an important warning to parents whose children are saying things like, *"If there were no insects in the world, humanity wouldn't last more than a few months."* The only proper response to this is "Wow!" since this is almost a direct quote from E. O. Wilson, the father of biodiversity and bard of the rain forests. Yes, the end of April traditionally brings Wildlife Week—sponsored, for more than half a century, by the National Wildlife Federation, during which millions of schoolchildren will learn the three key reasons why our imperiled rain forests must be saved: (a) rain forests are exotic and unique places where amazing and strange animals live; (b) many scientists think destroying rain forests would drastically change world weather patterns; and (c) rain forests are the source of the primary nutritional requirements of our children, sugar and chocolate. Herewith, in honor of Wildlife Week, a glimpse of fascinating rain forest critters your teacher won't tell you about:

Treetop tarantulas. Yes, huge hairy spiders hang over your head in the beautiful Peruvian rain forest . . . such as the pink-toed tarantula. No, tarantula bites aren't fatal, but they can cause pain and swelling in an entire limb! Males are small, inferior creatures who must be very careful during their love dance, or the female, who is much larger and has giant fangs, will gobble them up. This is an excellent lesson in the battle between the sexes: Males are nutritious snack food! "The male spider isn't worth much after he's helped propagate the species," says Gary Hevel, curator of the insect collection at the Smithsonian Institution.

Giant bug bombs. If you've seen the movie *Arachnophobia*, that's what Smithsonian scientist Terry Erwin does in real life: fires giant insecticide bombs into the treetops, then watches millions of insects fall dying into large funneled jars. Scientists believed there were one million types of insects in the world until Erwin came up with more than 800,000 beetles in the rain forest—and almost 30 million species of insects.

Heat-seeking snakes. The fer-de-lance sounds like something served with tea and petits fours, but it is actually a fatally poisonous six-foot pit viper that can sense your body heat in the darkness, long before you see it.

How Smart Are Gorillas?

Koko, a young female gorilla, learned 645 signs in American sign language and was able to discuss past events, which only humans were thought capable of. Other gorillas who have taken the Stanford-Binet IQ test in sign language have scored eighty-five to ninety, nearly identical to that of an average human child.

How Can I Prevent the Nation's Number-One Health Problem for Children, the Dog Bite?

With spring in the air and dogs out of the house, it's time for "Wild Things" to address your dog's number-one image problem and your child's most likely health problem: a dog bite.

Yes, dog attacks are the most commonly reported childhood public-health problem in the United States, exceeding the instances of measles, whooping cough, and mumps combined. According to the Humane Society of the United States, two to three million dog bites are reported to local authorities each year, with millions more unreported. Sixty percent of all dog attacks are against children, and 85 percent of the nine to twelve Americans each year killed by dogs are children.

Scared yet? Don't be. As with almost all problems involving dogs, you can see the cause in the mirror when you're shaving or brushing your hair each morning: you. This assumes your dog isn't a Border collie and doesn't do either in front of a mirror.

"It's not that dogs are Cujos waiting to happen, waiting to go crazy," says the Humane Society's Rachel Lamb. "In almost every case of a dog attack, you can find a human reason—one that could easily have been prevented." Here's how:

End your dog's sex life. By spaying and neutering your pet, you dramatically decrease the chances it will bite anyone, according to master dog trainer Brian Kilcommons, author of *Childproofing Your Dog*, an excellent guide to safely managing the dogs and children in your life.

Be as nice as your dog. Rover is already a perfect companion waiting to happen—it's up to you to live up to his legendary standard. Never play aggressive games with your dog, such as wrestling or tug-of-war or "siccing" Fido on your friends. Train your dog, socialize him heavily, and provide lots of attention. Dogs tied in the backyard or exiled to the doghouse are much more likely to become aggressive. License and vaccinate your dog, and don't allow him to roam.

One baby at a time. Don't get a new puppy to raise with new baby. "Save yourself the stress and exhaustion," Kilcommons advises. Instead, wait until your child is at least four, maybe five. When choosing a dog, remember, Kilcommons says, "Dogs bred to work closely with man and for low levels of aggression are better family dogs than those dogs developed for their fighting, killing, or aggressive prowess." Adopting a mutt is, of course, not only *the right thing to do* but often provides a mellower choice than the purebred. Purebreds lead the nation's biting charts. Beware of once wonderful family dogs, such as the golden retriever and cocker spaniel, who can be overaggressive because of overbreeding.

Last bite: For free brochures and more tips on dog-bite prevention, write the Humane Society of the United States, 2100 L Street NW, Washington, D.C. 20037.

What's a Family Pet That Will Not, Under Any Circumstances, Kill the Children?

One of the hallmarks of childhood is the First Pet. In our society today, parents are looking for a First Pet that can broaden a child's horizon and teach him about faraway cultures, such as the Burmese python. Strange as it may seem, in this sophisticated age, there are still some people who are afraid of a twenty-foot snake as wide as a tree trunk. It doesn't matter how many times the trained professional pet-shop owner says, "Properly cared for and confined, this is a perfect pet for your child." It doesn't matter all the educational things a child can learn in *The Columbia Encyclopedia* about BURMA or PYTHON:

Python (pi'thon, pi'thun). ". . . nonvenomous constrictor snake found chiefly in the tropical regions. . . . It climbs and swims expertly. It kills birds and mammals on which it feeds by squeezing them in its coils. . . . The reticulated or royal python of Southeast Asia may reach a length of thirty feet or more."

"Wild Things" recommends a simpler First Pet for young children not ready to handle cats or dogs, such as Ant Farms and goldfish. These are ideal First Pets that (a) cost a pittance, (b) are easy to care for, and (c) recall your own childhood in a misty glow, like a late-night rerun of "The Wonder Years."

Ants

"Ant Farm" is the registered trademark of Uncle Milton Industries, a once awesome monopoly that has sold fourteen million farms since the 1950s, but it has its competitors today. If you buy a competitor, make sure the ants will burrow during the daytime, like the Ant Farm's California red harvester.

Age of child: Child should be seven to eight years old. Younger children tend to shake up the Ant Farm, killing the ants. Just feed 'em a few times a week—a fragment of apple, a piece of meat, anything—and watch 'em work 'round the clock, without vacations or health benefits.

Amazing fact: The world's ants outnumber the world's people. They are the most numerous insect. World ant population: 10,000,000,000,000,000.

Worst scenario: The ants will die from too much sun or freeze to death in the cold. If someone opens the Ant Farm tube, they run out and bite, but it doesn't hurt much. Your Ant Farm ants will live several weeks to several months—it's anybody's guess, depending on how old they are, which is also anybody's guess. You just can't pick up an ant and tell how old it is.

Parents will say: "Better Junior stares at ants than at Beavis and Butt-Head."

Goldfish

Goldfish cost as much as a stick of gum (twelve cents apiece) and make good, small (one to four inches), easy-to-care-for pets for infants and toddlers. You can keep your twelve-cent goldfish in a bowl with no filtration. A ten-gallon tank will run about $50. Goldfish cost about $50 a year to keep. They live ten years, unless of course you have a cat.

Age of child: Children under one year love the colors and movement of a goldfish. The best goldfish for children is a young one—about two inches long. Five-year-old children can care for goldfish themselves.

Feed goldfish once a day. Goldfish food is available in pet stores. Use bottled water if tap water is chlorinated. Change water in an aerated tank once a month; nonaerated, once a week.

Life lesson: Staring at goldfish may help sensitize infants to living things more than, say, staring at a video or mobile. Taking care of goldfish is an excellent way to teach an older child responsibility and awaken him/her to nature.

Amazing fact: The Chinese domesticated the simple dark carp centuries ago—one of the first pets—and turned it gold with careful breeding. Goldfish now come in every imaginable color and have strange tails, double and triple fins, and bulging eyes.

Worst-case scenario: They could go belly-up.

Parents will say: "This won't possibly live ten years in our house."

Why Are Hamsters So Popular, Since They Bite When You Pick Them Up?

This is one of the great mysteries. Hamsters are incredibly popular pets. But the fact is, hamsters confront you with a classic catch-22: If you don't handle them and play with them a lot, they bite. If you pick them up during the daytime to play, they bite. Why? "Because they're sleeping," says Rachel Lamb. "They're nocturnal animals. They exercise all night and like to sleep during the day without being disturbed, like most people. A gerbil or guinea pig often makes a better pet."

The Turtle

The best starter turtle is the box turtle, a hardy, easygoing, docile tortoise whose only possible downside is that he will live one hundred years. The tortoise is about $30 to start and costs run about $80 a year, which may change depending upon inflation in the twenty-first century. Get a four- or five-inch turtle, which is about a year old. At age sixty, the turtle will zoom to its full size of six inches.

Age of child: Children should be at least eight, old enough to appreciate the slow, easygoing charms of a turtle. Turtles need to be fed only every other day. They need a warm area (being reptiles, they can't provide their own heat) and a good source of light in order to grow healthy shells. Turtles can show remarkable displays of affection, such as rapid blinking.

Life lesson: No creature in millions of years has figured out how to get a turtle to come out of its shell when it doesn't want to, so a child, too, must learn patience and respect for a different type of creature. Children become very attached to their turtles, whose heads come out of their shells when they see their keeper coming, or even will lie on a child or let a child stroke their necks. Turtles like to be read to, especially García Marquez's *One Hundred Years of Solitude*.

Amazing fact: True, turtles may seen less formidable than *Tyrannosaurus rex*, but turtles are as old as the dinosaurs and succeeded where the dinosaurs failed.

Worst-case scenario: Child uses knife blade to pry turtle from shell. Hasn't worked once in a billion years. Turtles are infamous for eye infections, and they can get soft shells if not kept in a well-lighted area.

Parents will say: "After the kids have grown up and gone to college, who will take care of Boxy?"

Hamsters

A short-haired hamster can be bought with pocket change—$5.99 or less. And you won't exactly break the bank for a long-haired (Angora) type for about $8.99. Cages range from $10 to $60, but some children prefer hamster aquariums, which start at $10. Food is about $1 a week. Cedar bedding costs about $2; change it once a week. Hamsters live three to six years.

Age of child: Children should be at least six years old. Food and water must be checked every day. Hamsters can go for a couple of days without care if you go on a trip. Hamsters are independent, like cats. Buy baby hamsters. Older hamsters may fight with each other and are more likely to bite children. Warning: Cats love to chase hamsters. Children should sit on the floor when playing with hamsters. If they drop a hamster while standing, the animal can die.

Life lesson: You don't need the "birds and bees" lecture with hamsters around. They're reproduction machines, gestating every twenty-one days. Yes, in three weeks, children can see the babies born. In another three weeks, the babies are independent.

Amazing fact: Hamsters exercise at night, putting enough miles on their wheels to go to the moon and back.

Worst-case scenario: If your hamster bites mercilessly during the daytime when you are trying to play with him, this is probably because you are *waking him up* and you probably should have gotten a guinea pig or gerbil, which sleep at night like normal folks. Hamsters are nocturnal animals, meaning they sleep all day and play at night. Another bad scenario: Your cat picks up your hamster one day before you do.

Parents will say: "Let Hammy sleep, play with the dog instead."

Rabbits

An excellent choice if your child is allergic to cats or dogs. Almost no one is allergic to rabbits. Rabbits cost from $10 to $40 from a pet store or farm and can be adopted inexpensively from an animal shelter. It costs $25 to $50 a year to keep a rabbit in commercial rabbit food, dried plants, and veggies. They live five to eight years.

Age of child: Children should be about seven years old, when they're calm and patient enough to let the rabbit approach for play. Children need to spend fifteen minutes a day caring for rabbits. Feed them rabbit food twice a day (a mix of dried plants, seeds, and vegetables), and let them out of the hutch to graze on grass in a closed-in area. The water bottle must be kept full and the hutch cleaned every day. Daily brushing is required.

Life lesson: Children will learn responsibility and patience caring for a rabbit. And they'll learn more about wildlife than a dog or cat can teach. A rabbit is used to living in a warren with many other rabbits and will become very lonely without a friend. The child will be the rabbit's best friend.

Amazing fact: Rabbits are Leporidae, which have two rows of top front teeth that never stop growing. Give your rabbit a small log to chew on to keep him from turning into Bugs Bunny.

Worst-case scenario: Rabbits are vulnerable to ear infections, glandular problems, and colds, not to mention birds of prey and cats.

Parents will say: "Who chewed up the phone cord again?"

What's the Most Popular Family Cultural Activity in the United States?

It's time to discuss America's pastime, which is not baseball but going to the zoo to see wild animals in startlingly realistic natural "habitats" fabricated of completely man-made materials, including fake rocks.

Yes, more Americans go to zoos than to all sporting and cultural events combined. Children especially love the zoo, where they can be imbued with a lifelong reverence for animals and learn astonishing truths about life, such as *"My parents don't know anything."* The myth of parental omniscience suffers some of its cruelest blows at the zoo. "Daddy, how many bones does a giraffe have in its neck?" "Mommy, what do tigers eat?"

The answers are easy: While your child is ogling the animal, nonchalantly *read all available signs, cards, and brochures.* Many of these signs are PG, but "Wild Things" gives the R-rated truth: A five-hundred-pound, eight-foot-long Siberian tiger will bolt down twenty to sixty pounds of meat at one sitting, then sleep beside its prey for several days, finishing everything, including the bones, which he can be heard munching for miles around. Giraffes have seven such bones in their necks, the same number as humans.

Here are more wild-but-educational things to do at the zoo:

Go during weather changes. It's a horrid, summerlike day with temperatures in the high eighties, then—bam!—a cold front moves in and it's a crisp, springlike seventy-one degrees. Yes, I know what you're thinking. "Dramatic temperature changes afford the best possible time to visit the zoo," notes Fred Koontz, curator of mammals at the zoo formerly known as the Bronx Zoo. "Animals are most active when the weather changes." The perfect time is ten o'clock Sunday morning, church time, when the zoo is empty and the bears at the Philadelphia Zoo, for instance, begin their highly instinctive activity of turning over logs, looking for Cheerios.

Sex and violence, naturally. As Charles Darwin often said, the point of life is, naturally, to have sex. This is difficult to tell children, so the zoo is an excellent *educational* way of discussing this timeless idea. When two-hundred-pound Galápagos tortoises mount each other in summertime and begin grunting, "Some parents say, 'Oh, they're just hugging' or 'They're wrestling' or other insane things," Philadelphia Zoo wildlife specialist Heidi Jamieson says. Be honest. "I heard once heard a three-year-old tell her brother, 'I saw the antelopes mating! The male put his front hoofs on her back, and then he put his penis in her vagina and she tried to get away.' This is exactly what happened. If people give proper names to things, it takes away a lot of the emotion." *Optional difficult truth: the carnivorous food chain.* "The first impulse of life," Jamieson notes, "is to eat and not be eaten."

Don't play football. True story: A father threw a football over the head of his eight-year-old son and into the tiger moat of the Philadelphia Zoo. Then Dad had some pals lower him by the armpits into the tiger moat so he could grab the football with his feet. Yikes! His buddies pulled this dunderhead dad to safety just as the five-hundred-pound Siberian tiger leaped twenty feet and recovered the fumble. "Don't play football with the tigers," notes Philadelphia assistant mammal curator Dave Wood. (In other words, stay out of the animal habitats.) There aren't many other health-safety issues to worry about at the zoo, unless you're allergic to bees. There are bees at the zoo, but they're not part of the collection.

Be Cliff Claven. Woo a child's attention the same way today's newspaper editors do, with a beguiling mix of Dull But Important Knowledge, such as, "Polar bears stay warm by trapping ultraviolet light in their hollow, transparent white hairs, providing a greenhouse effect," and Truly Alarming Facts, such as, "One tablespoon of king cobra poison is enough to kill 165 people, while a single bite from Australia's euphemistically named small scale snake can kill 250,000 mice."

In a pinch, remember, the most popular zoo animal for children under five is . . . the squirrel! True, the elephant and the bear came out tops in a Bronx Zoo survey of children. But youngsters, the researchers found, are most excited when they start to squeal, "Look, Mom, there's a squirrel!"

How Do Polar Bears Stay Warm?

Each of the bear's apparently white hairs are hollow and transparent. Ultraviolet light from the sun travels down the core of each hair, is absorbed by the bear's coal-black skin, and trapped by the hair like a greenhouse glass. The polar bear also has a tough hide and a blubber layer four and a half inches thick. *Editor's note:* At eight feet tall, seven hundred pounds, polar bears also stay warm by eating two-hundred-pound seals, which they can pull through a tiny hole in the ice with one great swipe, breaking every bone in the seal's body.

How Strong Are Gorillas?

The dominant male gorillas are six feet tall, five hundred pounds, and said to be as strong as the ten strongest men.

How Many Teeth Does a Crocodile Have?

A Nile crocodile's enormous jaws hold seventy razor-edged teeth—each replaced as many as forty-five times in a lifetime. So one crocodile could go through 3,150 teeth!

Why Is the Beaver Called the "Ward Cleaver" of Animals?

Compared to, say, the pesty, flighty raccoon, the beaver is a model of domestic behavior. He works around the clock on his dam and rushes to repair it if a storm damages the structure. Unlike most mammalian males, who run off with the youngest available member of their species, the beaver keeps himself busy, busy, busy in all seasons helping Mom and the kids with domestic tasks.

How Deadly Is the King Cobra?

One bite from an eighteen-foot king cobra can kill a person in fifteen minutes. A whole *tablespoon* of the king's venom can off 165 folks.

CHAPTER 11

REALLY WILD THINGS

JEFFREY DAHMER'S PETS,

CRICHTON AND SPIELBERG'S DINOSAURS,

SPACE JELLYFISH, SOLDIER BEARS, AND WHY ANIMAL

TEAMS NEVER WIN THE SUPER BOWL

How Did Jeffrey Dahmer, the Son of Sam, and the Boston Strangler Start Their Careers with Pets?

When I was a child, I tried to study all of nature under a magnifying glass, specifically to see if ants would burn up under the noonday sun. (They didn't.) My good friend Chris recalls sticking firecrackers down ant holes. We were just being "boys."

Now, "Wild Things" hardly condones such behavior, but it's not the kind of stuff, the experts tell me, that should have a parent worrying, "My child shows such disregard for life I'm afraid he'll become the next Jeffrey Dahmer. Or the next Richard Nixon." No, it's when you find cat and dog body parts in your neighborhood that you should truly worry.

I passed out of my ant-torture period when my father awed me with stories about Albert Schweitzer, the great humanitarian who, as I recall, shared his bacon with ants. Schweitzer once said, "Anyone who has accustomed himself to regard the life of any living creature as worthless is in danger of arriving also at the idea of worthless human lives."

Schweitzer was wiser than probably even he knew: Albert DeSalvo, the "Boston Strangler," who killed thirteen women in the sixties, had, in his youth, trapped dogs and cats in orange crates and shot arrows through the hole. David Berkowitz, New York's "Son of Sam," killer of thirteen people, had previously shot a neighbor's Labrador retriever. Childhood friends of Jeffrey L. Dahmer, killer-cannibal of at least fifteen people, recall seeing in Dahmer's backyard in 1975 the head of a dog impaled on a stick. Richard Allen Davis, recently charged with kidnapping and murdering Polly Klaas in Petaluma, California, had an early pattern of animal abuse as well.

We know it's not pleasant to read, but these men may never have made the headlines as killers of human beings if we knew what we know today about the link between animal abuse and human cruelty. The criminal "Hall of Shame" is filled with people who as children did nasty little things to pets; if their parents or teachers had seen the warning signs or known how to counsel them, history would be different.

"One of the most dangerous things that can happen to a child," the great anthropologist Margaret Mead has said, "is to kill or torture an animal and get away with it."

Animal abuse is not just a warning sign of a future adult criminal—it's a signal that a child is living in a deeply disturbed home environment and needs help. "Animal abuse by any member of the family, whether parent or child, often means child abuse is going on, too," says Randall Lockwood, psychologist for the Humane Society of the United States.

Here's what parents and teachers can do: Educators and guardians of youth must recognize that any child who abuses animals is in need of immediate help. (All states require teachers to report suspected animal abuse or neglect.) If a child describes animal abuse in the home, the school counselor and psychologist should be immediately notified. The local animal-welfare agency should also be notified to check up on animal care in the home. If there is no such agency in your area, call the police. Early intervention on animal abuse can prevent child abuse from happening—or stop child abuse from occurring. Establish a task force in your school to break the cycle of animal abuse—children who won't talk about being abused themselves will often come forward to talk about how their pets are mistreated.

Law-enforcement agencies are discovering these connections firsthand. Again and again, according to Eric Sakach, the Humane Society's West Coast cruelty investigator, "the police are learning that your local dogfight or cockfight is a likely place to meet lots of people with warrants outstanding for their arrest" for arson, drug charges, gambling, murder, and other crimes.

For more information on how to spread the word in your community, write to the National Association for Humane and Environmental Education, 67 Salem Road, East Haddam, Connecticut 06423.

Why is NASA Always Sending Helpless Critters, Like Tadpoles and Jellyfish, into Space?

To watch them throw up. This is a true story. NASA is obsessed with NAUSEA.

Our national space agency, which has forgone for the time being the search for Intelligent Life in the Universe, is obsessed in the nineties with the cosmic mystery: Why does everything we send into space get sick?

After sending more than one hundred people, several dogs and monkeys (the monkeys refused to eat), dozens of rats, and hundreds of insects into space (the ants died), NASA has found the ideal astro-animal. It even has the perfect name: the moon jellyfish.

This harmless round critter has a lively existence unimpeded by a brain or active emotional life. Its ocean milieu closely resembles the weightlessness of space. It is one of those mute and very ancient creatures classified as Cnidaria, that phylum family whose low-key reunions always include the freshwater hydra, sea anemones, and coral—as a whole, the dumbest living things on Earth. And it *normally* throws up everything it eats.

On June 5, 1991, the brave (to anthropomorphize quite a bit) 2,478 who flew on the space shuttle *Columbia* represented the lowest forms of life ever to travel in space. A largely unrecognized great day for the Cnidaria. Press accounts callously rounded them off to "2,500 jellyfish in space."

That was the historic flight during which astronauts tried to make themselves vomit by staring at fields of dots in rotating domes to simulate the sensation that their heads were spinning one way, like Linda Blair's in *The Ex-*

orcist, while their bodies spun in the opposite direction. The twenty-nine rats on board were allowed to circle the earth 146 times undisturbed until they landed in California and were beheaded, generating far more protest mail than the poor jellyfish, who got only one letter on their behalf. The baby jellyfish pulsed in plastic sandwich-style bags attached to syringes that, with one touch by vomiting astronauts, released chemicals to speed their growth into jellyfish puberty, kill, and pickle them. After a week of this, some of the moon jellyfish appeared to be swimming in circles but otherwise, remarkably, never showed any signs they had left Virginia.

This was very encouraging. "Jellyfish seem to be good space travelers," said Dr. Dorothy Spangenberg, biologist and jellyfish expert at Eastern Virginia Medical School in Norfolk, Virginia. "They took the blastoff and reentry very well."

It's also good news for our national goal of colonizing Mars, which right now appears to be an impossible dream. Here's the rub, for years a deep NASA secret: Space flight makes at least one in two astronauts hideously ill. Blood from the legs rushes to the head and chest. The face bloats, signaling an emergency order to discharge excess fluid— the technical term for the release of monstrously large blobs of cold space-sweat that ball up like mercury, roll around like Jell-O, and break off into space-cabin orbit. The heart literally shrinks. The feeling is similar to 120 days of Earth bed rest—except back home you can't drown in space-suit vomit.

The jellyfish, which have statoliths similar to human otoliths, will be studied to see how their gravity receptors were affected during the flight. Space-sickness is the big space issue of the nineties, the main impediment to space exploration. It's probably caused by conflicting signals: Without gravity pulling on the otoliths (literally, "ear stones"—gravity sensors that look like white sand) in the middle ear, your ears say, "I'm moving." Your eyes say, "No, I'm not." Your stomach says, "AAAARRRRGGGG." NASA's goal is to develop an anti-nausea pill. Something we can pop on red-eyes to the Red Planet.

How Michael Crichton Made Millions on *Jurassic Park* by Cooking Up a Dinosaur Recipe

We recently finished rereading *Jurassic Park*, Crichton's gripping sci-fi novel in which once-extinct velociraptors hop around like giant birds, are as intelligent as apes ("Harry, the blonde is running out the back! You go garrote her while I watch the patio door!"), bite like *Tyrannosaurus rex*, and generally spoil a nice theme park by ripping everyone's guts out. This is, of course, family entertainment, part of Hollywood history as a Steven Spielberg megamovie.

Crichton, the six-foot-ten California doctor-turned-writer, took the idea of cloning extinct dinosaurs from a group of California and Montana scholars everyone laughed at, made a fortune off their concept, and gave the scholars a few lines of credit on page 400 of *Jurassic Park*. This is the kind of opportunism for which Crichton slayed the Japanese in his subsequent best-seller, *Rising Sun*, but Dr. George O. Poinar, Jr., whose brilliant discovery made *Jurassic Park* possible, shrugs it off. "I have no hard feelings . . . it was a very interesting book."

It's also theoretically quite possible that we could create a dinosaur theme park (in which, we know, something would go *horribly wrong*), says Poinar, a paleontologist at the University of California at Berkeley. In 1982, Poinar and his wife, Dr. Roberta Hess, made an astonishing find: a gnat, embedded in a forty-million-year-old chunk of amber, so well preserved that the scientists concluded its DNA might have survived. Then, in 1983, Poinar, Hess, and physician John Tkach, members of the Extinct DNA Group everyone laughed at, were sitting around Tkach's Montana home chugging beers and laughing at themselves when Tkach said something like "Hey, what if we brought those monsters back!" (Tkach is a dinosaur nut who has gone on digs with Montana paleontologist John Horner, the model for Alan Grant in *Jurassic Park*, but receives no credit in the book for his idea.) Charles Pellegrino raised the notion in *Omni* magazine in '85, and more folks laughed. Crichton laughed all the way to the bank.

Poinar has even cooked up a *recipe for a dinosaur* that has not been tested by Julia Child and under no conditions should be tried at home. INGREDIENTS: (a) Find a bead of amber that contains a bloodsucking insect from the age of dinosaurs. (These are very rare, but check your engagement ring carefully for dark brown specks.) (b) Extract and copy genetic material, using a new laboratory technique called *polymerase chain reaction* (PCR). (c) Inject into embryo of an alligator. (d) Wait until it hatches.

"There is a race on now among a number of people throughout the world trying to get dinosaur bones and insect blood," Poinar said, "and my feeling is that within a year or eighteen months, someone will have a little snippet of dinosaur DNA."

After that, only two things will keep *Jurassic Park* from becoming real. First, it will be impossible to find the complete dinosaur genome—all the DNA—so "we'll need DNA repair kits," Poinar said. Second, biologists have yet to perfect cloning an individual from a single cell. Oh, and scientists have never found amber-embedded insects from the Jurassic Period, 190 million years ago making *"Jurassic" Park* impossible. Insects have been found from the Cretaceous Period, 65 to 140 million years ago. "The book should have been called *Cretaceous Park*," Poinar said.

Do Rats Have Feelings, Too?

The British are way ahead of us on important "green" issues, such as rodent and spider emotions. The Royal Society for the Protection of Cruelty to Animals in early 1993 prosecuted a woman who tried to mail home her pet spider, Boris, on grounds of extreme cruelty.

Then, the RSPCA won a lawsuit against a homeless woman for abandoning her pet rat on the grounds that rats have humanlike feelings too. According to *The People's Agenda* (a newsletter by an anti-animal rights group), Lisa Chapman was fined $120 and will have to pay $75 in court fees for leaving her pet rat Ziggy for six days with only a piece of cheese. Chapman, who is without a job or shelter, said, "I didn't actually abandon him. I had no choice." RSPCA superintendent Mick Flower explained the prosecution: "Who is to say that cruelty to one species is less of a crime than cruelty to another? We take the view that cruelty is cruelty."

Auberon Waugh, a writer for London's *Daily Telegraph*, said he understands this to mean "we cannot slap a fly or a wasp that lands on our forehead."

New Mammal Found in Lost World

Scientists led by John Mackinnon of World Wildlife International in 1992 discovered a new mammal, a horselike creature, in the jungles of Vietnam. "There have only been a handful [of new mammals discovered] in the last hundred years," Mackinnon gushed. The *New York Times* reported this rare mammal discovery, but a far more interesting newspaper, the *Weekly World News*, took it to a different level. THE MISSING LINK! STONE-AGE FAMILY FOUND ALIVE IN LOST WORLD! the tabloid blared. APELIKE NEANDERTHALS AMAZED BY A SCIENTIST'S CIGARETTE LIGHTER! "Our guy didn't see any of that," noted Lou Bayard of the World Wildlife Fund in Washington, D.C.

Whales Can Sing, but What Are the Lyrics?

Whales sing in great booming, creaking basses that make a marvelous accompaniment to the cello, but what are the lyrics? ("Jonah was a bellyful, then came Melville"?) What are they thinking with all that gray matter?

"Whales have the largest brains on earth, brains every bit as complex as our own," says Diane Ackerman, author of *The Moon by Whale Light*. "They have culture, and they have language. They sing songs that obey the kinds of rules one finds in classical music. . . . Why does it sing? What do the songs mean? Almost everything about the whale is a tantalizing mystery."

Whale songs are set to the rhythm of swells in the oceans, whale scholar Roger Payne has noted. Whales move so slowly and majestically that humans can barely interpret their *playing*—a whale's sense of time is so different from our own. Humpback whale songs can go on for months—the same monotonous (and possibly very complex) sounds repeated endlessly.

Some scientists speculate that whales (which include dolphins and porpoises) are using their big brains for *Star Wars* acoustics—sonic clicks that read distances and mud texture, even count edible fish. But bats perform equally complex tasks with brains smaller than a pea. So the rest of that gray whale matter, Payne suggests, must be used for important social tasks, such as cheating or making myths.

Infant humans require about a third of their body metabolism just to run their fancy brains—the same is true of infant dolphins. Mammals don't evolve intricate, expensive brains without good reasons vital to survival, but what the whale is thinking, Payne says, "Nobody really knows."

How Can a Parrot Be Smarter Than a Three-Year-Old Child?

Meet Alex, the world's smartest bird, an African grey parrot whose intelligence is dazzling scientists at the University of Arizona.

Alex doesn't just parrot human speech. He thinks in abstract concepts. He communicates easily with people. He understands questions and makes reasoned replies. When he's bored he throws his toys angrily around, clearly, if nonverbally, communicating, "I've seen all these before!" When he's hungry, he says exactly what he wants to eat, such as, "I'd like some cashews, please."

He identifies objects, materials, colors, shapes; understands the ideas of similarity and difference, bigger and smaller and "middlest"—a difficult concept for children.

Shown a felt triangle, rawhide square, toy truck, and five-sided piece of paper, Alex was asked, "Which object is five-corner?" "Paper," he said. Asked forty-eight such questions on shape, Alex got forty-eight right. He developed great affection for Irene Pepperberg, his owner, and learned human speech from her instantly.

Little is known about his background, although he probably comes from a broken family. (Divorce is common in parrot societies.) Somehow Alex, who is silver-gray with dark gray wings and measures about a foot to the tip of his black-red tail, ended up in a pet shop in Chicago. No one understands fully how his brain works, but it is clearly radically different from a human's—he has very little cortical area (cerebral cortex) and in some way processes information through a large striatal area.

What's so special about Alex? Nothing.

Pepperberg, a University of Arizona ethologist and Alex's owner, believes he's a parrot of "average" intelligence, no smarter than the eight other birds in his pet-shop cage. Her research shows that parrots are much smarter than has been supposed, with brainpower that may equal that of chimpanzees or dolphins—and are just as smart, in many tests, as a three- to five-year-old child.

What Animals Have Fought in War?

We must never forget animals in war, just as we remember veterans every year on Veterans Day. "Wild Things" fondly remembers a legendary World War II fighter named

Wojtek. Wojtek was strong and brave and liked beer and women, but he was different from his fellow soldiers in that he was a bear.

In many other ways, though, Wojtek, who fought for the Polish army, was just one of the guys exhibiting, for instance, an obsession for women's underwear. Wojtek, whose exploits were immortalized by London's Imperial War Museum, "had a weakness for women's underwear and once helped himself to the washing line of a female air-force unit," which did *not* lead, as far as we can tell, to any of those unfair jokes about the Polish army.

Anyway, nothing good happens to bears in war. Or to pigs, such as the Nazi pig rescued from a sinking German cruiser. Or the duck mascot for the Royal Scots Fusiliers who drowned in a shell-hole in World War II. Even today there are reports of donkeys and dogs strapped with bombs in the Middle East, and dolphins trained by the U.S. Navy to detect Persian Gulf mines. The good news is that modern "Nintendo warfare" requires fewer and fewer animals. This is no reason, however, to forget the brave horses, dogs, pigs, camels, mules, cats, goats, elephants, and pigeons who have served in wars since 1450 B.C., including:

Lassie, the parachute trooper. "Lassie" is the code name for collies, who were so sweet no army has ever been able to teach them to bite the enemy. This didn't stop Rob, a collie mix, from making more than twenty parachute jumps behind enemy lines for the British air force, faithfully serving as his unit's patrol and guard dog in World War II.

The pigeon who saved one hundred soldiers. When spies learned that one hundred Allied soldiers in an Italian village were targeted for a bombing raid, a carrier pigeon named Joe flew sixty miles with the warning that saved the day. Later Joe was whisked by U.S. Embassy car (giving new meaning to "passenger pigeon") to the Tower of London, where a British major general hung a medal of valor around his neck, almost knocking the poor bird over. Joe was the only American to win Britain's Dickin Medal for animal gallantry and heroism in combat in World War II. (Pigeons flew off with thirty-one of the fifty-three medals awarded.)

The patriotic poodle too old to fight. In World War II, twenty-five thousand of our nation's pet dogs were volunteered by celebs and commonfolk to serve in the "dogs for defense" movement. FDR himself enlisted Fala. But one day an old woman brought her aging poodle to the canine recruitment office. Phyllis Wright, U.S. warden of war dogs, humanely sent the pooch home. "That was a big part of her job," says Humane Society spokesperson Rachel Ward, "making sure the bigger and sturdier dogs got picked."

The terrier who jumped out of helicopters. A homeless waif, Rats attached himself to British army units in Northern Ireland and became the only dog marked for death by the IRA. He trotted at the head of patrols "and gave everyone heart failure by leaping out of helicopters thirty feet from the ground," says Jilly Cooper, author of a book on war animals. "But as a morale booster he was without equal." Forced to retire with half a tail and bullets lodged throughout his brave little body, Rats was honored with a full-dress parade. Six soldiers were kept busy answering his fan mail.

Help honor the forgotten U.S. vet. Did you know that thirty thousand dogs have served in four U.S. wars, and many were simply left behind when American forces left Vietnam, yet they don't have their own memorial in Washington, D.C.? To help rectify this injustice, write Joseph J. White, a Vietnam vet and former military dog handler who heads the National War Dogs Memorial Project, P.O. Box 6907, Jacksonville, Florida 32236.

Here, Rover!

Ever wonder where dumb, cliché dog names like Fido and Rover came from? Thank the Father of Our Country—George Washington helped popularize "Rover," which he named one of his hunting dogs. And Abe Lincoln had a Fido. In the eighteenth and nineteenth centuries these names still bore some trace of originality.

What Happens After Dog Owners Die?

According to many old dog stories and Disney movies, when you die your faithful pooch lies whimpering by your side. According to urban myth, your cat, being a cool, aloof carnivore, will slowly begin to nibble away at your remains.

Sadly, the opposite is true. According to cat expert Victoria Voith, there are numerous American-newspaper accounts of dogs that have eaten their owners who died alone in their homes. Hey, what do you expect of a book called *Wild Things*? Candy-coated truths? Cats, it turns out, are faithful felines, our true best friends. They let a sleeping owner lie.

Why Are Elephants Going on Rampages in Circuses and in the Wild?

Faithful reader Teresa Johnson of Ambler, Pennsylvania, sent us this question along with this true headline from the *New York Times*: WILD ELEPHANT KILLS 44 VILLAGERS IN INDIA.

Teresa wondered if this development in India was some-how connected to the horrible death of an Oakland, California, zoo trainer whose last words, as a formerly docile 10,500-pound pachyderm smacked him with his trunk, were: "Get back! Get back!" Theresa's question was: What the heck is going on with our beloved elephants?

After a careful investigation I can confirm that (a) yes, there is a serial-killer pachyderm on the loose in India; (b) our circus and zoo elephants, which are said to have the intelligence of six-year-old children, are increasingly rebel-ling—after waiting twenty-three patient and submissive years for the trainer to turn his back—with the ele-phant statement "I want to be in charge now," which is not a pretty thing to witness; and (c) do not make any travel plans to the northeast Indian villages of Thelamara, Muslim Char, or Butamari unless you want your morning headline, PHILLIES SHOCK BRAVES IN 10TH, to be replaced by: ELEPHANT KILLS 12 MORE (Reuters, Oct. 1), or ENTIRE ELEPHANT HERD TURNS BAD. The villagers of Assam are not alone in this terrible problem. In Sri Lanka, famous for its beautiful women and fine tea, the Xinhua News Agency once re-ported: ELEPHANTS KILL VILLAGER AFTER ALCOHOLIC DRINK IN SRI LANKA.

In Asia the problem is simpler to define than to fix: Hu-man beings are increasingly encroaching into elephant for-est areas. "There isn't enough land for the elephants and the villagers," said Sri Lanka sugarcane farmer Tikiribanda Ratnayake, who sleeps every night in a tree while ele-phants below smash villagers' mud-and-thatch huts to find food and water. A vast sugarcane operation has closed the elephants' traditional route to the Yala water hole. Some elephants searching for water unfortunately have devel-oped a taste for the local moonshine, *goda*, the vast consumption of which by an angry elephant leads to a guaranteed front-page story. As a growing human population makes more contact with elephants, people are awed by the great beasts' memory and capacity for revenge. In Assam a lorry driver who gave some bananas to a wild elephant found his way blocked for weeks afterward by the entire herd demanding bananas or sugarcane for safe passage. In Dacca, Bangladesh, an elephant whose calf was knocked down by a locomotive blocked the next train and destroyed the engine by butting it for fifteen minutes with its head.

Elephant trainers in the United States are learning the same lesson Asian villagers have long known: Elephants are astonishingly intelligent—laugh, cry, practice elaborate social rituals—and don't soon forget intrusions on their habitat or freedom. Training elephants is the most dangerous job in the United States, according to federal statistics. (Of the six hundred U.S. elephant trainers, one is killed, on the average, each year, but that figure is rising alarmingly.) This was tragically underscored when Axel Gautier, the world-famous elephant trainer for the Ringling Brothers/Barnum & Bailey circus, was pushed down and stomped from behind while videotaping performing elephants near Gainesville, Florida. But trainers remain in awe of their increasingly unruly charges. "The elephant isn't in a zoo by choice," says John Lehnhardt at the National Zoo in Washington, D.C. "It's wrong to punish it."

The last, dying words of trainer CharLee Torre, twenty-five, after being kicked and crushed by Tillie, a four-ton Asian elephant at the Lowry Park Zoo in Tampa, were "Please don't hurt the elephant." Tillie was humanely removed to a breeding farm in Florida, leaving Minyahk, forty-two, the other Tampa zoo elephant, so lonely and upset that he was moved to a zoo in Springfield, Missouri. Minyahk, whose Hindu name means "Remover of Obstacles," was given the more politically correct identity C.C, the initials of a famous Missouri weatherman from the fifties.

How can you help? The Asian elephant is an endangered species that may be extinct in twenty years. To help, write the World Wildlife Fund, 1250 24th Street NW, Washington, D.C. 20037. Circus or zoo elephants often become aggressive or hostile after years in captivity, and are destroyed. Riddle's Elephant Breeding Farm & Wildlife Sanctuary in Greenbrier, Arkansas, offers a home for such elephants. To help, write Riddle's at P.O. Box 715, Greenbrier, Arkansas 72058.

Why Do Animal Teams Never Win Big Games?

This explains why the American Football Conference always gets humiliated in the Super Bowl by the National Football Conference. AFC animal teams like the Denver Broncos, Buffalo Bills, and Miami Dolphins don't have a chance against NFC "people" teams like the Dallas Cowboys and San Francisco Giants.

Take it from us, Vegas Mike. No 800 numbers. No refunds. No doubts. Here's the "Wild Things" NFL Sunday Special: Never bet on an away dog . . . or cat, eagle, tiger, or any animal team. Animal teams don't win. Critter mascots bring on choking, or curses—who the heck knows? It just happens. Need proof?

We did our homework. Only four of the twenty-six Super Bowls have been won by animal teams—the Dolphins, twice, the Colts, and the Bears. Eleven of twenty-eight NFL teams sport animal mascots, yet, with few exceptions, most of them are historically lousy—Falcons, Seahawks, Eagles, Cardinals, Lions, Colts.

The historically great NFL teams are *people* teams that fall into three categories: Cowboys and Indians (Cowboys, Redskins, Chiefs), Blue-Collar Workers (Steelers, Packers), and Mythic Mean Dudes (Raiders, Giants).

The same goes for college football. An amazing 55 of the 106 Division I-A teams are animal teams, more than half. But only three of the top ten all-time winning percentage teams are animals—the Michigan Wolverines, Texas Longhorns, and the Penn State Nittany Lions. Only twenty of the sixty-five college football national champions have been animal teams, this despite the fact that the most popular college football mascots are the eagle, wildcat, and tiger, which makes sense, as cats and birds evoke the power and speed we wish of our football players. Or, at least, they ought to.

According to the College Football Association, among two thousand college football teams, the seventy-two eagles, sixty-eight tigers, and a host of canines and clawed animals like bears far outnumbered laborers, Indians, natural weather conditions, and satanic figures. But the great college teams are people teams, inspired by figures of ethnic or regional pride: the Fighting Irish, Sooners, Buckeyes, Cornhuskers, Volunteers.

Take pro baseball, pro basketball, pro hockey. The rule applies across the board. The dynasties belong to people teams: Yankees, Dodgers, Celtics, Lakers, Canadiens. The doormats are the Tigers, Cubs, Bulls (for most of their history), Red Wings.

The reason is very simple. Mascots—taken from the

Middle Latin word *masca*, or magician—have been used since ancient times to give people protection from evil spirits and their like. But mascots work better if they're human. The subconscious boost of a metaphorical cowboy is a lot easier to summon than your basic abstract ocelot. It's a theory.

Almost 15 percent of all Division I-A college football teams are Wildcats, for instance, and most of them, like Northwestern University, which unfortunately is my alma mater, have been scientifically proven to be lousy. Your average Wildcat scatback doesn't even know exactly what a wildcat cat is. If he looks it up for a psychic boost he finds he could be any number of medium-sized North American cats, such as the lynx, serval, and, yes, the ocelot. He finds confusion. Too bad, since a wildcat can run more than twice as fast as a blue-collar worker and return a kickoff ninety-nine yards in about four seconds. 'Bout as fast as you can say, "Go, Wildcats, go!"

What Was the Meanest Dinosaur That Ever Lived?

The "Utahraptor," discovered just in time for *Jurassic Park*. This is a true Hollywood story.

Steven Spielberg wanted to scare the wits out of people in *Jurassic Park* with the velociraptor. He wanted to create the meanest dinosaur ever—a "superslasher," twice the size of a man, that walked on two legs. The problem was, it just never existed that way. The real velociraptor was a lot smaller, only slightly bigger than a man. Spielberg created a fictional monster.

Then, in July of 1992, just before the movie came out,

researchers in eastern Utah discovered partial remains of a velociraptor *just like* the vicious meat-eating dinosaur that ran amok in *Jurassic Park*.

Mike Perry, executive director of a Colorado-based group that helped confirm the discovery, said the Utahraptor was twice as large as earlier-known raptors, which were slightly larger than man. "We have confirmed what Spielberg wanted to do," Perry said.

Paleontologist Jim Kirkland sent Spielberg a cast of the claw to confirm that there was indeed such a monster—the twenty-foot, one-ton Utahraptor with a single, fifteen-inch slashing claw.

"The armament is so formidable on this thing—a deep skull, serrated steak-knife teeth . . ." Kirkland said. It was, he said, the meanest dinosaur ever, far more dangerous than T. rex, and hunted in packs. The "superslasher," he called it. Just in time for the movies.

What's the Largest Living Thing on Earth?

Today's leading candidate is . . . a mushroom omelette. Sure, as children we learned it was the blue whale, which could pack 130 tons into a 113-foot-long body. Then, in the late 1980s, paleontologists found a dinosaur to rival the whale and called it "supersaurus." Then, bigger still, the seismosaurus, up to 120 feet long and 18 feet high at the shoulder. In the spring of 1992 a team of Canadian and American scientists found what they called the largest living thing extending across thirty-seven acres in northern Michigan—a giant mushroom. Most of it, thank God, beneath the surface. In 1993 scientists reported a forest of simple birch was even bigger, many square miles of trees all connected—as *a single organism*. Makes you wonder who all those trees are whispering about.

Cruelty Doesn't Pay

From our new and expanding file, "Cruelty Doesn't Pay," we bring you two more cautionary tales of pet abusers gone really bad: Anthony Casso showed his early insensitivity to living things as a teenager shooting pigeons on rooftops in Brooklyn in the fifties. Casso, fifty-two, grew up to be a Mafia boss and achieved the number-one ranking on the FBI's Most Wanted list for allegedly ordering eleven successful mob hits. (Whether these were "stool pigeons" is unclear.) *Animal People*, a new monthly newspaper "for people who care about animals," reports on Casso in its police blotter, along with accused Ohio serial killer Thomas Lee Dillon, who moved from cruelty to cats and dogs to allegedly shooting three hunters, a jogger, and a fisherman. When he was finally apprehended, he was found shooting at road signs.

CHAPTER 12

ENDANGERED
THINGS

IN WHICH THE DARWIN OF OUR TIME EXPLAINS
HOW THE WORLD COULD END,
THE VERY LAST UH-OH BIRD SINGS A SONG OF LOVE,
AND A BATHHOUSE SLUG GOES EXTINCT AND
UNDERSTANDABLY NO ONE CARES

Who Is Often Called the "Darwin of the Twentieth Century"?

The most exciting thing about being an animal columnist is getting to meet legendary figures like the father of the theory of evolution, Charles Darwin. Yes, you say, being an alert reader, but Charles Darwin is now 184 years old. This is technically true, but it does not lessen the impact of meeting the "Twentieth-Century Darwin," who is Edward O. Wilson, the great Harvard University biologist, currently only sixty-four. We met with Professor Wilson in

Washington, D.C., recently as he stood outside the Dirksen Senate Office Building, chatting with an ant. We're not making this up.

"Hey, little buddy," Professor Wilson said. Wilson was rushing to a meeting with Montana senator Max Baucus and Rhode Island senator John Chafee to point out that more animals are going extinct these days than at any time since the dinosaurs, but that would wait because congressmen, Wilson said, are not as important as ants. "Ants are the little ones that rule the world," the professor said. "Without them, the major mammals would crash to extinction in a matter of months and humanity not long afterward." This is not the kind of thing journalists usually cover until it's *way too late*, but the ant is also nature's hardest worker and with Labor Day being in the news ants are *extremely timely*. Herewith, the "Wild Things" Ant Appreciation Guide:

Don't go splat! Most ants are harmless and in fact *essential to our survival* as a species. The best ant story we know occurred several years ago in Washington, D.C., in the seventh-floor office of the president of the World Wildlife Fund, or WWF, which, as you might expect, is a very large organization devoted to saving animals. An ant was scurrying across the president's desk, so the president, being a normal human being, lifted her palm and was about to go *SPLAT!* Fortunately, E. O. Wilson himself was sitting across the desk, and he cried out, "No! I don't think the president of a major wildlife organization should be responsible for wiping out the only known member of a new species." Wilson scooped the ant up and later identified it as a *new species of ant*, which had crawled out of a corner plant that came from Miami. The professor later found another ant of the same species in the West Indies.

Farmer ants. Read on and amaze your friends, who will give you the fond nickname "Cliff Claven." Large leaf-cutting ants (Wilson's favorite) chomp leaves to small bits and pass them on to tiny leaf-cutting ants no bigger than a period (actual size of leaf-cutting ant: .). These period ants seed mulched leaves with some fungus and grow crops to feed the *entire colony*. Lacking any kind of farming ability, there are five species of North American slave-making ants who kidnap whole colonies of weaker, more talented ants, imprison them, and force them to do things we cannot repeat here.

Burial ants. Last week, Jill, who is my wife, noticed on the kitchen floor an ant busily carrying a dead ant on what appeared to be its shoulder and disappearing somewhere under the TV set. This reminded us of the touching last part of *Lonesome Dove*. When ants die, they are covered with a glandular chemical that signals the burial ants to come pouring out of the colony and carry the dead away to the ant burial grounds, which most people have somewhere in their kitchen. This is also true.

What Serial Killer Is Stalking Guam?

It was one of the great ecomysteries of our time: What happened to the birds of paradise (in this case, the Pacific island of Guam)? By the 1980s scientists realized almost all the birds were gone, and no one knew why. The chilling answer was the exploding, alien population of the brown tree snake, which was wiping out forest birds and shrews, rats, poultry, and even pets. (And even some small children.) This eco-horror story is told in a much-praised book, *And No Birds Sing: The Story of an Ecological Disaster in a Trop-*

ical Paradise by Mark Jaffe, an environmental reporter for the *Philadelphia Inquirer*.

This is everyone's problem, Jaffe notes. Alien species pose a global threat to ecosystems and biological diversity, from the Great Lakes, which are being choked by the zebra mussel, to the Florida Everglades, which are under assault by Australian trees and African fish, to name just two. "Wild Things" heartily recommends *And No Birds Sing* as an ecothriller about a biodiversity serial killer.

How Can I Save Endangered Species in My Backyard?

Yes, spring is the time to weed, seed, fertilize—and save endangered species in your backyard! You may feel power-less to protect the thirty types of deadly scorpions in the Peruvian rain forest, but you can play God on your own green acre, reintroducing orioles, owls, hawks, butterflies, and other nice family-type critters. This will teach your children priceless lessons about nature, imbue your soul with the deep peace once felt by Henry David Thoreau, and further your children's illusion that you are omni-scient. Here's how:

Lawns are barren ecosystems. The typical suburban spread is a couple of species of grass, some earthworms, robins tugging the earthworms, a cat, a dog, a few kids. Throw in the obligatory tree or two and some bushes and insects, and you've got maybe forty to fifty different species and no place for up to one hundred endangered birds (e.g., orioles, warblers) and other creatures. To change all that . . .

Don't nuke the clover. Clover was a respected part of American lawns until the lawn-chemical companies per-suaded us it was a weed, says Craig Tufts, backyard specialist with the National Wildlife Federation. Clover attracts nice rabbits and groundhogs, symbols of spring and fall; caterpillars that become butterflies; bees, which pollinate your garden; and kids combing for four-leaf clovers.

Summon the astonishing owl. This is simple: Plant trees! "The old woodland suburbs are home for three to five times as many species as new developments," Tufts says. Oaks harbor two hundred or more plant and animal species, from insects to birds to squirrels. Squirrels and chipmunks attract hawks and owls, which children love and which can seize a speeding rat in total darkness and down it in one gulp. "That's like a two-hundred-pound man swallowing a forty-pound beaver whole," marvels zoology student James Key. This happens quietly while everyone is asleep, so you can still nurture the childrens' book fantasy of the nice wise owl until the kids are old enough to learn the truth about nature.

Let the grass go. Check with town hall and your neighbors first. But a backyard meadow, sown with wildflowers and native plants, attracts an astonishing diversity of life. Kids love to learn about frogs, lizards, and harmless snakes. It's backyard biodiversity!

Save the birds. Of the 330 species of songbirds—robins and hummingbirds, to name two—that build spring nests in the Americas and migrate south for the winter, 70 percent are in decline. To help save them, plant trees, recycle paper, and write to the Bird Conservation Specialist, The Smithsonian Migratory Bird Center, National Zoological Park, Washington, D.C. 20008, for a $5 book with many other ideas.

Keep kitty inside. This is good for your cat and really good for the 19 million songbirds in Wisconsin that would still be alive if nice kitty hadn't been let out last year. "Cats are great, but they were never part of our ecosystem—only bobcats [are]," Tufts says. "Europeans introduced them, and they're out of control." Cats have made whole species of Pacific Island birds extinct.

What's the Greatest Threat Facing Humanity?

It's not what you think. According to a national poll of twelve thousand adults by Defenders of Wildlife, the public thinks the greatest threats to the fate of the Earth are the environmental problems that dominate the news—acid rain, toxic waste, and pollution. These are small potatoes compared to the Four Modern Horsemen of the Apocalypse in the view of U.S. Environmental Protection Agency scientists. These are the biodiversity crises caused by the disappearance of species, the loss of habitat, ozone depletion, and global climate change.

All these problems are us. Some scientists believe that the fact that humanity descended from tribal, territorial, sex-and-aggression-crazed primates makes us the worst possible caretakers of the planet. Thus, we are rapidly overpopulating, polluting, burning, and bulldozing jungles and woods and streams and countless natural habitats. This raises the possibility, E. O. Wilson speculates, that a law of evolution "may be that intelligence extinguishes itself."

Is Twentieth-Century Mankind, Like the Dinosaurs, Living in an Age of "Great Extinctions"?

Yes. Look at it this way: you live in interesting times.

There have been five great extinctions in the past 440

million years. We are, some scientists believe, on the threshold of the sixth. The last great extinction came 66 million years ago when a giant meteor strike, or megavolcano eruption, many scientists believe, made the Earth uninhabitable for the great reptiles and countless other creatures. At the current rate of destruction of wildlife and habitat, some scientists maintain, as much as 20 percent of all species on Earth will be extinct within thirty years, forming the Sixth Great Extinction. Says E. O. Wilson: "I cannot imagine a scientific problem of greater immediate importance for humanity. . . . The number of species of plants and animals in the world is being reduced at a rate . . . as high as ten thousand times faster than in prehistoric times."

Experts don't foresee an eco-apocalypse of sci-fi–horror-movie proportions, but frogs, amphibians, and 20 percent of all fish are disappearing, and half of all songbirds are already gone. In environmental hot spots around the globe, we will increasingly be mourning the loss of whole categories of living things.

What Medical Miracles Came from Endangered Species?

Thanks to the endangered rosy periwinkle plant in Madagascar, Hodgkin's disease and lymphocytic leukemia have become largely curable. Taxol, drawn from the Pacific yew, contains one of the most promising anticancer drugs known. Cyclosporine, taken from an obscure Norwegian fungus, is the powerful immune-suppression agent that makes the entire organ-transplant industry possible. A drug used to treat rheumatism and contusions was derived from the saliva of the vampire annelid worm.

What Will Happen if the Socorro Bathhouse Sowbug Goes Extinct?

Nothing.

It's traitorous for biologists to admit, but some species losses just don't seem to harm the big picture. The very concept of biodiversity—the complex layering of perhaps more than 100 million species of plants and animals without which human life would never have evolved—is that each part is vital to the whole.

For example, biologists are now learning there are "keystone species," the removal of which causes an ecosystem to unravel as if a seam has been pulled on a sweater. No one knew, for instance, until a certain species of Pacific otter all but disappeared, taking with it the fish, the birds, and practically an entire ecosystem, that the otter was a keystone species upon which the entire community depended.

The Socorro bathhouse sowbug is not such a species. It is one of those disgusting slimy pill bugs you find under rocks. And there's apparently only one left, E. O. Wilson says, lying by "a warm stream in one abandoned bathhouse in Mexico. If it were to go extinct, I don't think even the ecosystem of the bathhouse would collapse."

What's It Like to Go 150 Years Without a Date?

This is the plight of the gentle gopher tortoise, the only tortoise indigenous to the southeastern United States and now an endangered species in Alabama, Mississippi, and Louisiana, where there are fewer than two hundred left, says Southeastern Louisiana University biologist Richard Seigel. The poor tortoise often goes a century and a half without even *seeing* a member of the opposite sex. Or, for that matter, the same sex. In the Depression, the gopher tortoise was a major food source for ordinary folks, who dubbed it "Hoover chicken."

Is the Northern Spotted Owl Really Endangered?

Myth-bashing time: The woes of the endangered northern spotted owl have used up several forests' worth of newsprint, involved two U.S. presidents, and sparked a national debate on endangered species. The only problem is, the spotted owl *isn't* an endangered species. It's a "threatened species," which is sort of the on-deck circle before "endangered" classification. The U.S. Fish and Wildlife Service listed 558 U.S. endangered species and 170 threatened species in September 1992. Biologists hate it when reporters say, "Gimme a Top 40 bound for extinction." ("Don't these press geeks understand we're being asked to play *God* here?") But there are at least 558 plants and animals that are a heck of a lot worse off than the 2,500 nesting pairs of spotted owl, such as, for instance, the Florida panther (thirty to fifty left in the Everglades). Of course, no one really knows how many endangered species there are. Scientists estimate one hundred unknown species become extinct every day, unseen.

How Can I Save the Rhino?

Go bowling.

Africa's ancient and noble black rhino is one of the most tragic of animals—in twenty years the herd has been reduced from 65,000 to fewer than 2,500 by poachers who sell horns to be made into dagger handles in Yemen and folk medicines in Asia. The best thing you can do, short of moving to Africa to devote your life to the cause, is . . . bowl!

Yes, more than fifty zoos in cities across America annually sponsor spring bowl-a-thons aimed to raise more than $100,000 to send to the Ngare Sergoi sanctuary in Kenya, haven for twenty-five black rhinos. To bowl or start a bowl-a-thon for rhinos, call your local zoo or write to Patty Pearthree, Bowling for Rhinos National Chairperson, P.O. Box 199026, Indianapolis, Indiana 46219.

Whatever Happened to the Florida Alligator, Valedictorian of the Class of '67?

In 1967 Americans saw *The Graduate* and heard, sung wistfully, "Where have you gone, Joe DiMaggio?" and watched in disbelief as the federal government released the first official list of endangered species in the United States—seventy-eight in all. What happened to the Class of '67 later in life?

The American alligator, the valedictorian, made a complete recovery. Forty-four species, such as the red wolf, California condor, whooping crane, and bald eagle, have stable or increasing populations due to Endangered Species

Act protection, while about twenty species remain in decline. Eight species probably have become extinct, according to an Environmental Defense Fund report, including the dusky seaside sparrow and the Hawaiian Kauai O'O bird, of which one male was left in the late eighties, singing joyfully to attract females. Poor guy hasn't been seen in years. The relative success of the Class of '67, the report argues, is reason enough for Congress to protect the Endangered Species Act itself.

How Can I Save Earthworms?

You're barreling down a summer highway, family van loaded with kids, beach balls, and vacation dreams, when you're alerted by the distress of a dehydrated earthworm on the grassy swale beside the roadway. You could just keep on going, burning up the fossils of deceased dinosaurs and polluting the planet, or you could stop. How the average 55-mile-an-hour driver can spot a prone roadside earthworm, we're not sure, but *Animal Alert*, a Connecticut newsletter, says earthworms are often stranded by the road in summertime and "they dry up quickly and die." The right thing to do, *Animal Alert* recommends (we're not making this up), is to "remove your credit card, scoop up the earthworm, and move it to a moister environment farther from the highway." You'll feel better for it.

Whatever Happened to Flipper?

Flipper went on to the great dolphin pool in the sky, but Richard O'Barry, who trained the dolphin star of the sixties

TV show, works with the World Society for the Protection of Animals in Boston to free captive dolphins. "So much that is wild and free has already been lost to us," O'Barry says. "We must leave these beautiful mammals free." There are hundreds of captive "entertainment" dolphins in the United States, but many countries are reevaluating the practice.

How Can I Save the Last Four Thousand Tigers?

There are only slightly more than four thousand tigers left in the wild, according to the Endangered Species Project. Taiwan is the biggest market for tiger parts for medicinal uses (a single tiger carved up can fetch $60,000, and a bowl of tiger-penis soup costs $320). For more information and officials to write to, contact the Earth Island Institute, Endangered Species Project, Fort Mason Center, E-205, San Francisco, California 94123.

Why Are a Third of All Known Living Things . . . Beetles?

This is true beetle mania. A British naturalist, asked what nature had taught him about God's plan, said, "God has an inordinate fondness for beetles." Yes, there are 340,000 different types of beetles, not to mention the estimated *ten million* different types of undiscovered beetle species in the rain forests. One-third of all known living things are beetles, for reasons unknown to man and unexplained by God. Beetles are, however, important. We know this much: If all beetles and other insects were to disappear, the forests would fade and most fish, reptile, bird, and mammal populations would crash to extinction for lack of food. "The earth would rot," according to one scientist. "Complex forms of vegetation would die off and with them, the last remnants of the vertebrates." That's us, pal.

How Do Zoos Serve as a Modern "Noah's Ark"?

With extinctions occurring at a rate unprecedented in the planet's history, zoos have been called upon to protect the future of entire evolutionary lines.

The days of collecting wild specimens are over. For the past decade, more than 90 percent of zoo animals have been born in captivity. Animals vanishing in the wild are thriving in zoos, whose highest purpose nowadays is to educate the public to protect threatened habitats so animals will flourish where they belong—in the wild.

Zoo breeding programs are credited with saving several species of feral dogs reintroduced into the wild and with giving birth to a whole new generation of the rare mountain tapir. Wyoming's black-footed ferret, of which there were only six left in 1985, has been saved by zoo captive breeding, as has Brazil's golden lion tamarin, a small primate, and the Arabian oryx, an antelope.

Captive breeding is part science, part "Dating Game." A committee of U.S. zoo curators recently spent three days discussing which tree kangaroo would make a suitable mate for a lonely heart at the Bronx Zoo, with emphasis on keeping the captive species' gene pool as close as possible to that of the animal in the wild.

Zookeepers are planning for the twenty-sixth and twenty-seventh centuries, according to Janine M. Benyus, author of *Beastly Behaviors: A Zoogoer's Companion*. Demographics experts say that the human population, which reached five billion in 1987, will be ten billion by the middle of the twenty-first century. Then our population will level off for five centuries, relieving the pressure on land and habitats that is driving animals to extinction. Then, zookeepers imagine, their precious banks of captive animals and frozen egg and sperm will repopulate a barren world. The voyage of the ark will be complete.

How Many Living Things and Endangered Things Are There on Earth?

This is the type of number that government agencies and wildlife groups are forever putting out, but the truth is *no one really knows.*

You wonder, Doesn't someone *keep count*? Aren't there, as the U.S. Fish and Wildlife Service says, *precisely* 558 endangered species in the United States? Aren't scientists named Edmund G. O. Johansen scouring the globe turning over rocks to find miraculous and rare rock-clingers they can name *Bacterius spiderus johansen*? These are media myths.

The fact is new species are being discovered *all the time*. Our museums are overflowing with heretofore unknown life; after a while it's so *boring* scientists don't even pop a cork when they become the first humans to set eyes on a living thing. They don't even have time to study documented species. Over 99 percent of discovered species, says E. O. Wilson in his astonishing book *The Diversity of Life,* "are known only by a scientific name, a handful of specimens in a museum, and a few scraps of anatomical description in scientific journals."

The truth is we have *no idea* how many wild things there are. A census of all living earthlings, says Wilson, "could be close to 10 million or as high as 100 million." There's just too much life to count!

In the nineteenth century, biologists thought the deep sea was lifeless. Crushing water pressure, no light. Real-estate nightmare. Who'd live there? Swarms of worms, crustaceans, mollusks found nowhere else on Earth—maybe ten million undiscovered animal species! Ka-jillions of other slimy things in the deep! Millions of insect species still unstudied on land! Millions of undiscovered bacteria living on the millions of unstudied insects!

Bergey's Manual of Systematic Bacteriology, updated in 1989, lists about four thousand types of bacteria in the world. Like the Palm Beach Social Register, the bacterial blue book conveniently excludes all manner of scum—the great mass of "silent" bacteria so vast and silent that some biologists call them "the Proletariat." (How bacteria are "silent" as opposed to boisterous party animals we will not attempt to explain in a family newspaper.) You think there's a single line in history books about the micro-proles? It's all *Escherichia coli! E. coli! E. coli!*—the elitist colon-dweller that converts food to feces.

Norwegian microbiologist Jostein Goksoyr went in search of the underclass and found four to five thousand new bacterial species—in a *single gram* of soil. Under his fingernail. "It is obvious," Goksoyr writes, "that microbiologists will not run out of work for a couple of centuries."

Just washing their hands. And making up names.

How Many Species Are Disappearing from the Rain Forests?

Tropical rain forests cover an area as big as the forty-eight states and are being removed at the rate of one-half of all of the state of Florida each year. As many as 100,000 species are disappearing each year.

What's the Most Doomed Population of Domestic Animal?

The mixed-breed dog. More than 8 million unwanted mongrels are killed each year in animal shelters, according to the Humane Society of the United States. If you want a dog, adopt a mutt.

How Many Species Go Extinct Every Day?

Seventy-nine, according to one study.

Thumbnail Census of All Living Things

Number of identified species on Earth: 1.4 million. Percent of species (excluding plants) larger than a bumblebee: 1 percent.

CHAPTER 13

Do the Right Things

HOW TO ADOPT A MUTT,

LEAVE A MILLION DOLLARS TO A CAT,

BE NICE TO MOM,

PREVENT UNWANTED PET PREGNANCIES,

AND AVOID ROADKILL

Why Should I Adopt a Pet from the Pound?

With apologies to the cast of *Carousel*, May and June are busting out all over and it's raining cats and dogs—litters are blooming everywhere for you to choose from. "Wild Things" has simple advice: *Don't.* Buying a puppy or kitten from a breeder often rewards the greedy, evil merchants of pet overpopulation. (Okay, so they're not *evil*, but we're trying to combine "Hard Copy" and "Inside Edition" tricks with National Public Radio wisdom here, so bear with us.)

Instead, save a cat or dog from the animal shelter—not

because it's the right thing to do, the cheaper thing to do, and will make you glow inside for saving a life, but because mixed-breed dogs and cats are often *better pets* thanks to the genetic miracle of hybrid vigor. Healthier. Mellower. Smarter. This is scientific truth, but you won't read it in our consumer society because mixed breeds lack *brand-name identification*. Yes, no one makes a buck off them, so no one touts their virtues. What you'll hear is, "Mutts are *just as good* as purebreds for some families, but of course *you don't know who the parents are*." (Subliminal message: Worry like heck. Come meet Chadworth's parents, who are, of course, the King and Queen of England. Naturally Chadworth costs ten times as much as a simple mongrel, but you get what you pay for.)

This line of reasoning works with a BMW 740. For $50,000, you get status *and* value. But it often doesn't work with dogs. Buy a purebred pooch for $500–1,000, chances are you've blown it, pal. You've bought a Mercedes with a Yugo under the hood.

The poodle can carry defective genes that produce abnormally shortened leg bones, displaced kneecaps, heart artery defects, degenerative eye retinas, teary eyes, diabetes, dislocated shoulders, epilepsy, behavioral abnormalities, and bladder stones. We've bred the bulldog's head so big and the Chihuahua's pelvis so small they cannot even reproduce themselves and require cesarean deliveries. For our pleasure and whimsy, we've made the noses and jaws of bulldogs, Pekingese, boxers, and Boston terriers so short they suffer obstructed breathing and pituitary cysts. Big dogs like Saint Bernards and Great Danes endure bone problems and shortened lives. Spinal deformities haunt the dachshund and basset hound because we've made their legs so short.

You can go right down the tragic list of the ten most

popular dogs in America: Labrador retriever (cataracts, kidney disease, bladder stones), German shepherd (eye abnormalities, cardiovascular defects, bad hips, aggression problems), the beagle (epilepsy, glaucoma, heart problems, spinal deformities, skin allergies). You get the picture.

What to do? Amazingly, mixes bear the positive traits of a breed—the shepherd mix, for instance, is noted for its loyalty and intelligence—without many of the genetic problems. Geneticists call this "hybrid vigor," which is the technical way of saying that a mixed-breed Irishman like Bill Clinton can become president.

So unless your purebred was developed by an extremely reputable breeder (who doesn't churn out litters willy-nilly, who cares more for the dogs than the money), it may well suffer from the genetic and temperament problems common to popular purebreds. Trust the random mating process you'll find at the pound. Trust Mother Nature. (Very simple test: Take the dog out in the back of the shelter. Play with it for half an hour. Have it checked by a veterinarian—the shelter's will suffice. If it's a healthy, friendly dog, you don't need to meet the parents. You're seeking a pet, not re-creating the Hapsburg dynasty.)

Here are ten ideal family dogs you can find at the pound that your children will love to identify:

1. *The black-and-tan dog (shepherd mix).* The most popular dog in the country. The number of humble black-and-tans in the country outnumbers the most popular American Kennel Club purebreds "like Oklahoma State batters your high school team," said Jacque Schultz, dog behavior expert at the ASPCA in New York. Amazing fact: Your "shepherd mix" may not have an ounce of actual shepherd blood. "Mate a Newfoundland with a Chihuahua, and after

ten generations you'll have what looks like a shepherd mix. Your basic dog," Schultz says

2. *The black dog (black Lab mix)*. Round. Hairy. Thirty-five to fifty pounds. Tail sticks out like the "automatic plant" you had in college and never watered. Unimaginably friendly. You'll never need a paper towel for spills with this dog around. Every neighborhood has one. Make that six.

3. *The brown dog*. Forty pounds, narrow snout, medium hair. Great companion. What all dogs looked like when people traveled in caravans—not Dodges but bands of hunter-gatherers. Also called "natural dog" or "perfect dog." What all dogs would look like if we let them choose their love partners.

4. *The golden white dog*. A golden retriever mixed with a German shepherd or sometimes a yellow Lab. A gorgeous, very popular type, gentle with kids, friendly to mailmen (unless they actually approach the house).

5. *Benji*. The terrier mix, Brillo hairstyle, comes in any color, 6 to 160 pounds (full-size Don King version).

6. *The shepherd-collie mix*. Lassie meets Rin Tin Tin, with the best of both worlds.

7. *The Border collie mix*. Border collies are wonderful farm workers. But they can be lousy house pets. They're too smart and have been known, very systematically and impressively, to peel the wallpaper from the kitchen unless kept very busy (say, herding a thousand sheep). The mellower Border collie mix has great wit but has never sent its owner back to the wallpaper store for the Laura Ashley and French Country books.

8. *The cockapoo*. This cocker spaniel–poodle mix is so popular it has almost become its own breed, which may lead to its downfall.

9. *The Lassie-Not.* An unkempt but irresistible collie mix with any patch of sable, black, brown, or white; a wavy coat; and a long muzzle—but never that true collie needle nose. Aka "Lassie, Go Comb" dog.

10. *The "Heinz" dog.* Any dog with an apparent "57 varieties" of parents can be a Heinz, but the classic Heinz is a hot-dog dog. These are incredibly outgoing sausage-type dogs that are easily identified as poodles, beagles, or dachshunds—after ten generations of random mating, or eight revolutions in a Cuisinart.

How Can I Pilot My Pet Safely Through the Unfriendly Skies?

For pet lovers planning a vacation, "Wild Things" recommends you *do not* fly Lassie along in the unfriendly skies. If your dog or cat meets an all-too-common tragic end like the golden retriever Floyd, who died of heatstroke in the 140-degree cargo hold of an American Airlines jet, you might learn that the law cares little for your anguish over the loss of this family member.

My dog Blue, for instance, is of incalculable value to our family, having provided eight years of companionship, protection, and love so strong that our three-year-old daughter cries when she leaves Blue behind for vacation. All this love comes at a remarkable bargain, considering Blue cost less than a family-size bucket of chicken ($7.20 at the shelter). Now a New York judge has decided Blue's true value: $7.20 minus depreciation, of course.

Yes, in one of those Cro-Magnon decisions reminiscent of the English common law that women were chattel, a federal judge in Manhattan ruled that Andrew Gluckman of

New York, owner of Floyd, the poor, doomed golden, was entitled to only lost-baggage compensation. He couldn't sue for anguish and loss of companionship.

Spokesmen for several airlines said they treat pets with great care, and relatively few pets are ever harmed during flight. But Rachel Lamb, director of companion animals at the Humane Society of the United States, says something else: Pet deaths on airlines are such an alarming problem that more than one hundred animals have died aboard airline flights since 1990. "We recommend you never transport your pet by air, unless absolutely necessary," Lamb says.

Here's how to increase your pet's chances of arriving alive if he or she *must* fly along:

• If you own a cat or small dog, take the animal on board with you. Contact your airline carrier to learn its requirements for this option.

• Use direct flights when traveling with your pet. More mistakes and delays in getting your pet off the plane occur during airline transfers.

• If you must put the pet in cargo, always travel on the same flight. Ask the airline if you can watch your pet being loaded and unloaded at the cargo hold.

• When you board the plane, notify the captain and at least one flight attendant that your pet is traveling in cargo. If the captain knows pets are on board, he may take special precautions to protect them.

• Don't ship pug-nosed dogs or cats, including Pekingese, chows, or Persians. "These breeds have short nasal passages that do not give hot air a chance to cool off before it reaches the lungs," Lamb says.

• To avoid temperature extremes in cargo, book early-morning or late-evening flights in the summer, afternoon flights in the winter. Don't fly pets during holidays, when rough cargo-handling is more common.

• Use a sturdy carrier with proper ventilation and room for the animal to stand up and turn around. Clip your pet's nails to protect against their hooking in the crate's door and holes.

• Don't feed your animal for four to six hours prior to travel, except for small amounts of water before the trip. Put ice cubes in the crate water tray. Don't give your animal tranquilizers unless veterinarian-prescribed for air travel.

• Fit your pet with two pieces of identification: a permanent ID with your home address and a temporary tag with your destination address. Carry a photo of the animal when you fly to help with identification if the pet is lost.

• If anything goes wrong during the flight, take your pet to a veterinarian immediately and get the exam results in writing. Then contact the airline, the U.S. Department of Agriculture (USDA, Animal Plant and Health Inspection Service, Washington, D.C. 20250), and the Humane Society of the United States (2100 L Street NW, Washington, D.C. 20037).

How Can I Leave All My Money to My Cats and Dogs?

Today's service journalism feature is: "Providing for Your Pets in Your Will" (Or: *Why your dog has followed you around all these years*). This is a true story: Tobacco heiress Doris Duke, one of the world's richest women, died recently at the age of eighty. Naturally, she left not a cent of her billion dollars to her adopted daughter Chandi.

As expected, Duke did, however, set up a $100,000 trust fund for her dog. "I am convinced I should have not adopted Chandi," Duke wrote in her will. "I have come to the realization her primary motive was financial gain." We wonder: Did this occur to Mrs. Duke *before* she gave the thirty-five-year-old Hare Krishna ex-belly dancer a Hawaiian estate or *after*? Whatever, the will had an entire page of good things to say about her dog, whose primary motive always seemed to be a Milk-Bone. The unnamed dog will live out its days in Duke's Beverly Hills estate with its own trust fund devoted to the "care, feeding, comfort, maintenance, and medical treatment of such dog."

Such Dog was one lucky canine, but is not, however, the world's richest pet. This title went to Viking, a German shepherd who inherited an entire block of real estate in Munich in 1971, according to the scholarly volume *David Frost's Book of Millionaires, Multimillionaires and Really Rich People*.

Anyway, unless you, too, are one of the world's wealthiest individuals and can afford the law firm of Cagey, Bully, Fearsome and Rich, "Wild Things" does not recommend leaving your fortune directly to your pet. What happens in these cases is you make the front page of your local newspaper as an eccentric, amusing and touching the hearts of everyone in town except your relatives, who sit around the kitchen table cursing your dog Bruno and pooling their money to hire a lawyer to take Bruno's bequest away. This often works, as Bruno appears in court and reveals that all he wants is a Milk-Bone. Perhaps the most famous challenged pet will was that of Edward Chester's of Queensland, Australia, whose six nephews, together with his sister, took grave exception to his leaving £42,000 (£144,574, or about $185,000, today) to his racing pigeons.

To avoid such confusion, Melissa Seide-Rubin, an attorney for the Humane Society of the United States, recommends you find a friend or family member "while you are still healthy and well" to commit to caring for Bruno after you are gone. Bequeath an outright gift of money to this person to take care of Bruno. Don't resort to trusts or fancy legal structures without a lawyer, as many state courts may not recognize animal trusts. If your pet is extremely old or ill, euthanasia upon your death may be the most humane thing to do. Do not leave your animals in the care of an organization or institution without carefully investigating first.

Finally, we are sorry to have to break this news, but *there is no cat old-age home*. Elderly women are forever calling the Humane Society asking for the name "of that cat farm in New England where my cat can go and be taken care of always," says Rachel Lamb. There are no-kill sanctuaries for cats, but they either have waiting lists until the next millennium or are dirty and overcrowded, Lamb says.

The Cat That Lost Its Kitty

Cat lovers are still mourning the case of Madame Dupuis, the famous French harpist who died in 1678 and left most of her fortune to her cats, providing thirty sous a week to be spent on the cats "in order that they may live well." Her greedy human heirs, a sister and niece, contested the will, which the courts overturned.

How Do All Species Take Advantage of Mom?

Yes, every May brings Mother's Day, when millions of Americans take a few moments to honor the most important person in their lives before leaving the kids with Mom and going to the movies. Everyone knows mothers (except Joan Crawford) are the most intelligent and wondrous creatures in all of nature, so naturally all wild things, blue whales to newts, take advantage of them.

Herewith, a roll call of nature's Great Moms. But first, you must go to a tattoo parlor and have this engraved on your shoulder: THERE ARE NO BAD MOMS. Whoa! Tell that to the piglets as thousand-pound Mom rolls over on them by accident. Sorry, junior! Or the cowbirds who dump their eggs in another bird's nest or the elephant seals who—whoops!—accidentally crush the little ones to death. Or the guppies gobbled up by Mom at birth. All would be candidates for Mom of the Year, according to Janine M. Benyus in *Beastly Behaviors*. "In the animal world," she says, "there's no such thing as bad parenting . . . the good parent award goes to every animal that manages to leave a successor."

Moms do everything. Talk about your second shift! To begin with, moms—cat or human or whale—have to make eggs, which in all species are 85,000 times larger than sperm and take a heck of a lot more energy to produce. "For the male, whose initial investment is minimal, promiscuity pays," Benyus says. Then Mom pours epic energy into the embryo and raises the young, whose first words in most species are "Where's Daddy?" All moms can say is, "Ninety-five percent of all mammals are nonmonogamous, dear," meaning Daddy is looking for another chickadee. "Assured that his genes are in good hands, he dedi-cates his energies to mating with as many females as pos-sible." (Don't judge harshly, Benyus says. This behavior is "adaptive and, therefore, beautiful.")

Turtles lay 'em and leave 'em. Frogs, salamanders, toads, and snake moms don't stay around to help with math homework. It's deposit the eggs and . . . have a nice life! Since both eggs and hatchlings are ready-to-eat predator snacks, moms produce offspring in staggering numbers, hoping a few will make it to kindergarten. Turtle moms are splitsville after laying their eggs on the beach, knowing the newborns will instinctively follow the rising sun into the sea. In Fort Lauderdale, alas, hatchlings sometimes head instinctively toward the nice round headlights on High-way A1A. Thanks, Ma!

Why Is Cat and Dog Sex a Bad Idea?

During the season of the birds and bees, "Wild Things" issues an annual urgent reminder that the youngest and most naive members of your family never be allowed to go unescorted to bars or have any sex at all. These are your cats and dogs. A life without sex is not a life without joy, a philosopher once said, but in any case April is Prevent-a-Litter Month, and "Wild Things" urges every American to practice total pet abstinence, which has recently become an important national issue. Here are four reasons to Just Say No to pet sex:

The pet holocaust. The Humane Society of the United States has called for a one-year voluntary ban on breeding cats and dogs to ease the "overpopulation crisis" of 110 million pets. "Responsible pet owners already spay and neuter their dogs and cats," said HSUS president Paul G. Irwin, "but many more refuse to recognize that by allowing their pets to have just one litter, they are sentencing millions of others. . . ." Of the twenty-seven million dogs and cats born in the United States yearly, twelve million are killed in shelters. Adopt a purebred dog from the pound (one in four euthanatized dogs is a purebred). Or: "If you can't decide between a shepherd, a retriever, or a collie, get all three in one dog," says Rachel Lamb.

Cats are breeding machines. Cleveland Amory's Fund for Animals is sponsoring a bill that will require all outdoor cats in California to be sterilized, and here's why: The average cat, left to its favorite, graduate student–style dating pattern (many sex partners for seven years) will produce in that time *420,000 unplanned kittens!* For a neutering fee of about $45, you'll save *one million lives* your cat could have produced in his lifetime. Take your receipt to *Time* magazine and nominate yourself for Person of the Year.

You'll still be macho. Men, veterinarians say, are the biggest opponents to "fixing" their male pets, apparently under some sort of guy-code that males of all species must be protected. "Fixing," is, indeed, a euphemism for "removing both ovaries and uterus in female pets and removing the testicles in males," says Philadelphia veterinarian Susan McDonough. That's the way responsible vets do it, she says, and "don't settle for less." This will not make your dog listless, fat, or unhappy, or prevent you from buying a red sports car and growing your hair extra long on one side to hide the thin part.

Prevent dog bites. Altering a male dog greatly reduces the chances he will bite someone, says master dog trainer Brian Kilcommons. Most dog bites, "by far," are committed by young male dogs (ages one to three) who haven't been altered, Kilcommons says. Why? "The wonderful world of testosterone," Kilcommons says. "Ask your wife about it."

Safe Sex for Dogs

Here's some big pet-sex news: The Humane Society of the United States now endorses early spay/neutering of cats and dogs, says Rachel Lamb. Puppies and kittens should be fixed as soon as they enter shelters, which "would save millions of pet lives" by preventing unwanted litters, she notes. Traditionally dogs and cats were "fixed" at six months for no good reason but tradition, says Susan McDonough, who fixes early and often at her Cat Hospital in Philadelphia. New research shows that spaying and neutering can be done safely at just a few weeks of age. Early fixing makes cats and dogs a little taller. "But they don't become giraffes or anything," McDonough states.

Why Shouldn't Dogs Be Left Home Alone?

Dogs who stay "home alone" don't fare as glamorously as Macaulay Culkin does in the movie, says the American Veterinary Medical Association. "Separation anxiety, brought on by changes in the pet owner's schedule, can result in destructive behavior," says veterinarian Wayne Hunthausen, "including excessive barking, clawing, house soiling, and chewing. The behavior can even be triggered by the sight of a suitcase. . . . Trash cans, cabinets, and bags of food are common targets." The AVMA recommends a slow break-in period for the pet, a $10–15-a-day pet-sitter, or a cat who doesn't care if you're there or not.

How Can I Get the Lead Out of My Birds?

Lead poisoning is an increasing problem in pet birds, *Bird Talk* magazine reports. Make sure your birds never have access to the following items (or remove them from the home): Tiffany lamps, stained-glass window frames, drapery weights, bullets, shot, pellets, some types of paint, batteries, paint tubes, plaster, putty, glazed ceramics, foil, linoleum, mirror backings, costume jewelry, leaded glass fumes.

How Can I Justify Giving Money for Abandoned Pets While People Go Homeless?

"Wild Things" often hears variations on this question from nonpet people, especially when millions of dollars is spent on a new animal shelter. Harvard biologist E. O. Wilson believes we need to express an innate love of other living things—"biophilia," he calls it—without which we are not fully human. An eloquent testimonial to this is being provided in Sarajevo, where many people have had to release their dogs, cats, and birds for lack of food, but others sacrifice to care for their pets amid shattered streets and bombed-out buildings.

One forbidden mixed-marriage couple, an Orthodox Jew and a Muslim who stay together against the law, took in an abandoned cat and a dog, who gave birth to seven puppies in front of their apartment building. Five of the puppies, the couple told National Public Radio reporter Scott Simon, survived because people brought scraps from their own rations—humanitarian rations, as the aid agencies call them. From the NPR transcript: Simon (interviewing): "There are some people . . . who might say given the fact that every human being here is suffering, to sacrifice for pets is just caring about the wrong things." Anna: "We are taking care of them because we feel that we need something to live around us. We are feeding the birds, too, because we need them around us. We are not evil . . . they remind us of peace, you know, everyday peace. We have to believe that we are going to survive."

Why Can't Pets Enjoy a Hershey's Kiss?

Because it's the kiss of death. Never give a cat or dog a Whitman Sampler or, even worse, real Godiva chocolate. Chocolate contains a chemical called theobromine, which is toxic to cats and dogs. Not to mention horses, pigs, chickens, ducks, and calves. We know of an eight-month-old Airedale terrier who died from eating bars of baking chocolate. And a two-year-old Labrador retriever who collapsed and died after downing cacao-bean shells. Both died of overdoses of theobromine, according to the *Journal of the American Veterinary Medical Association*.

Reports *JAVMA*: "The concentration of theobromine in the shells may very considerably (0.19 percent to 2.98 percent), depending on the variety of cacao bean and on the amount of fermentation. Poisoning of dogs with cacao products has been reported with food containing as low as 0.2 percent theobromine." Dog and chocolate lovers beware. The risk is greater the purer the chocolate.

How Can My Pets Survive the Holidays?

You think the holidays are stressful for *you*—they can kill your pets. Here, in memory of Stan and Bob, David Letterman's two dogs that died horrible holiday-related deaths (see chapter 6, "Whatever Happened to Letterman's Dogs?") are ten ways to be extra nice to your pets during the holidays, i.e., by preventing their untimely death:

10. *Don't* give a pet as a gift to a child. "When a child receives a pet as a present . . . the specialness of an animal is lost when it is given along with toys," says Marc Paulhus of the Humane Society of the United States.

9. *Do* give a gift certificate that can be used at the local animal shelter. If your children pick out their own pet, they will care for it better.

8. *Do* put the Christmas tree in a room that can be closed off. Pets can pull the tree down on themselves when you're away or asleep.

7. *Don't* use Christmas-tree tinsel or glitter. Cats are attracted to shiny things, such as your personality, but tinsel can be fatal if swallowed. Keep cats away from string, ribbon, or wrapping paper, too.

6. *Do* use low-voltage lights or keep lights high on the tree. Cats and dogs are prone to chewing electrical cords, which is not a good thing.

5. *Do* vacuum up tree needles as they fall and keep pets' water dishes full so they won't drink the tree water. Pine needles and even tree water can be toxic to pets.

4. *Don't* leave holiday chocolates lying around open. Chocolate can be fatal for cats and dogs. Ditto for Halloween and Valentine's Day.

3. *Do* send away for the free Iams brochure, either *You and Your New Kitten* or *You and Your New Puppy*, if you get a holiday pet. Call the Iams Pet Nutrition Center & Hotline at 1-800-525-4267, extension 44, Monday–Saturday, 9 A.M.–8 P.M. Eastern time for the brochure and other pet-care questions, too.

2. *Don't* feed your dogs all the fatty trimmings from a Christmas roast. This is how Letterman's dog Stan died. "Too much ham just killed him," Letterman said. Eating an excess of fat can cause an inflammation of the dog's pancreas that causes digestive enzymes to misfire and can bring on vomiting, dehydration, and death.

1. *Don't* let your dog eat the Prestolog or Duraflame log or any such product. This is how Bob died, from tumors associated with eating a Prestolog, Letterman said.

Halloween: A Bad Day for Black Cats

Halloween has traditionally been a dangerous time for black cats, who are at increased risk of being harmed by holiday pranksters, according to the American Humane Association. We're *serious*. "People are more likely to harm black cats on Halloween because of their mythical association with witches and the holiday itself," said Michael Kaufmann, humane-education coordinator for AHA. To keep your pet safe from Halloween pranksters, keep him indoors. Keep dogs or cats confined to prevent them from slipping outside or becoming aggressive when you greet trick-or-treaters at the door. Give pets dog biscuits or catnip toys as their Halloween treats.

How Can I Avoid Turning Nice Small Animals into Roadkill?

The "Wild Things" staff loves Memorial Day. Folks fire up the barbecue, chase down the beer. Head to the shore in the roadster and—oops—kill a few squirrels and chipmunks on the way. This, of course, is not funny: Memorial Day weekend is not only the deadliest time for motorists, it's Black Friday for rabbits, who were very intelligent creatures until 1903, when they began to pass the word that Fords were just large foxes to be outrun. (The *Opossum Handbook for Highway Safety* disagrees on this point: "Crouch low and the Headlight Bird will fly harmlessly above you.")

Sadly, animals in the road are the second leading cause of single-car accidents, after drunk driving, says the Humane Society of the United States. The annual roadkill carnage includes 1.5 million cats, 500,000 other small animals, like dogs and chipmunks, and 350,000 deer. Oh, and the one hundred humans who die in deer-car collisions. Most of these tragedies could be easily prevented if motorists would remember this easy tip—*Deer Crossing is not a town*—and post this on their refrigerator.

Cats think a Mercedes is a large mouse. Predator cats hunker down by the road to avoid being seen and—bam!—bolt out into the road. To avoid the cat, just *swerve in the direction the cat came from*. "Cats usually run in a straight line across a road. They rarely stop and double back," says Merritt Clifton, editor of *Animal People* magazine. Otherwise, keep a steady speed. Cats hunt in roadside ditches and may spring out if you slow down.

Bears don't back down. Bears, cows, and moose are so big and unafraid of anything they just hold their position against advancing automobiles. They're hard to see at night, and if you hit one you're almost as likely to die as they are. Warning: Bull mooses have derailed railroad cars and will attack your car.

Stop for chipmunks. Chipmunks, rabbits, and squirrels avoid predators by rapidly changing directions, Clifton says. Slow down and let them scamper away or they'll keep zigzagging ahead of your tires.

Don't slow for skunks. Skunks, like porcupines and armadillos, are so well armed against predators they tend to step into the road to look directly at the weird lights. Drive steadily around them. Don't give 'em time for curiosity to kill 'em.

Assume dogs have no sense. Sometimes you hear someone say proudly, "My dog has car sense." What are these people thinking? If you see a cat, squirrel, chipmunk, ball, or another dog cross a suburban road, assume a dog is chasing it and has forgotten his car sense, if he had any.

How Can I Liberate My Neighborhood Killer Whale?

If you're renting the onetime hit move *Free Willy*, take it from us: *Don't try this at home.* Naturally, Hollywood got it all wrong.

The "Wild Things" staff was wondering exactly how the average person is supposed to liberate a captive killer whale when after careful research of the cetacean order, we determined these creatures can weigh nine tons and are twenty-one feet longer than the cargo area of a Dodge Grand Caravan with all the seats removed. This causes several logistical problems, namely, you have to take the groceries out first.

If you ever hope to free a killer whale: (a) Don't use

credit cards or home phones, because any idiot who read *The Firm* knows the FBI traces that stuff, so why didn't Tonya Harding's bodyguards figure it out? (b) Take along this handy "Wild Things" guide:

Don't believe Free Willy. Willy's rescue "is totally fictitious and would be very harmful to a real killer whale," says Humane Society whale biologist Naomi Rose. Yes, as in *Free Willy*, it's okay to simply lift the whale from its tank with a sling and winch that can hold up to nine tons and transport the whale in a truck on a foam-rubber cushion for a short drive. But Willy's car-wash visit is a "pretty unlikely" way to wet down a whale, who does not encounter fresh water or hot wax in his native environment. Finally the rescue truck's mad, wooden-gate-splattering dash from the bad guys and right into the water "would so traumatize a whale, it might not survive." Keiko, the actor-whale who played Willy, relied on a stand-in robot whale for this dangerous scene.

Fly whales first-class. Carefully lower the whale from its sling into a large tub half-filled with seawater, then slide three or four large adult whales into a Boeing 747 with the seats, flight attendants, and all three-ounce bottles of Chivas Regal removed. That's how Sea World, which owns eighteen of the twenty-one captive killer whales in the United States, transports them. Sea World, Rose says, is an excellent whale caretaker, but "the point is no one should be caretaking them. They're just too big." The thirty killer whales that have died in captivity in the U.S. were terribly bored, subject to disease, and died at an average age of twelve. In the wild, killer whales live forty years on average and can live until eighty.

Don't swim with killer whales. Killer whales are the smartest and most predatory of all whales and dolphins, Rose says. They hunt in groups, have forty powerful teeth shaped like highway cones, and swallow harbor seals and other whales whole (thus the quaint nickname "killer whale"), and can defeat great white sharks in combat.

Free Keiko! Irony being Hollywood's favorite theme, Keiko remains captive in Mexico in far worse conditions than most American captive whales endure: a small tank, too-warm water (he's shed his blubber layer), a poor filter system, and a skin condition, evident in a rash clearly seen in the movie. Activists are trying to free Keiko, but in real life it's much harder. "We're trying to find a place to quarantine a four-ton killer whale for six months. This is not easy."

How Can I Get Involved with an Assistance Dog?

Paul Kerins, forty-four, of Long Beach, California, wrote us after reading about Perry and Prudence, two heroic dogs who make life livable for Tim and Cindy Bunge, a young handicapped couple in Centreville, Maryland. When I called Paul one night, he was unemployed and sounded down, having lost his construction business to help care for his sick mother before she passed away and, while caring for her at home, broke his ankle so badly he could barely walk.

"After reading your column I decided I wanted to devote my life to training assistance dogs to help the handicapped," Paul told me. "I love dogs, and I'm good with animals, and I want to make a contribution. I think this will make a difference in my life." I suggested Paul call the Delta Society in Renton, Washington, the experts on animal-human interaction, who can help anyone learn to train his or her dog properly to serve sick or handicapped people. You can write The Delta Society at P.O. Box 1080, Renton, Washington 98057-9906 or call (206) 226-7357.

How Can I Help Solve Pet Overpopulation?

Sadly, only 14 percent of pet owners get their cats and dogs from shelters, according to *52 Simple Things You Can Do to Help End Pet Overpopulation*. The Humane Society of the United States publishes this forty-page booklet, full of tips from the straightforward (spay or neuter your pet) to the savvy (go on cable-access TV to talk about pet overpopulation) to the sneaky (stuff airline seat pockets with pamphlets). For information on the booklet, contact the Humane Society of the United States.

CHAPTER 14

LIFESAVING THINGS

HOW DOGS LICK YOU OUT OF DEEP COMAS,

BIRDS LOWER YOUR CHOLESTEROL,

AND RABBITS EASE ARTHRITIS PAIN

How Can Pets Bring You Out of a Deep Coma?

What is this, the *National Enquirer*? No, it's all true—too-good-to-be true for your basic big-city newspaper, which specializes in horrible news.

Take the case of Donny Tomei, eleven. On November 4, 1991, Donny was hit by a car and suffered a serious head injury. The boy lapsed into a deep coma. For two weeks the medical staff at New Haven Hospital in Connecticut tried every conventional treatment. Still Donny lay unconscious in a nest of IV tubes, unable to open his eyes or utter a word. Doctors speculated he might never recover. Half the people with such serious head injuries die.

It was time to try anything. It was time to bring in a miracle dog. Therapy animals are often used to treat coma patients, says Maureen Fredrickson, deputy director of The Delta Society, a nonprofit group in Renton, Washington, that trains and licenses therapy animals. "There have been dogs and cats and rabbits who go into a community's hospital and the animal lies on the bed and the therapist takes the hand of the person in a coma and strokes the animal and it brings them back," she said. "A miracle is rare, but it does happen."

It was time for one more. Enter Donny's dog, Rusty, a frisky chow chow–collie mongrel puppy, into Donny's hospital room. Donny loved the puppy, whom he had adopted from a shelter. Racing by the medical staff, the puppy leaped onto Donny's chest and licked him in the face. Donny Tomei opened his eyes for the first time in two weeks, and smiled. "Bad Rusty," he said. These were the first words the boy had spoken since the accident. Dr. Charles Duncan, his neurosurgeon, stammered, "Donny is clearly not in a coma now."

The health benefits of dog companionship are well known, but even dog experts had never heard of such a thing.

Hundreds of cards and balloons and more than $3,000 in donations for Donny arrived, and many people sent pictures of their dogs. Pet stores offered dog food and a lifetime's grooming for Rusty. "This is really a boy-and-his-dog story," Duncan said.

Only half the survivors of such injuries make meaningful recoveries, Duncan stated. But Donny's condition began to improve markedly after his family got permission to bring his beloved mutt to the hospital. That day, after uttering his first words, he also ate for the first time since the accident.

Pets Can Save Your Life: A User's Guide

Once upon a time, on the streets of West Philadelphia, Jay Hart was beaten, partially paralyzed, blinded in one eye, and left for dead.

Now, in the hills of Chester County, he joyfully rides a horse—to learn to walk again. Only a sheepskin separates Hart from the rolling back muscles of Buffalo Bill, a large black-and-gray gelding who is one of ten "therapy horses" at the Thorncroft Equestrian Center in Malvern. On the same trail, children with brain injuries, multiple sclerosis, and cerebral palsy ride for increased coordination and for self-esteem.

"Horseback riding really strengthens the muscles of the back and stomach for balance and posture and trunk control," says Terri Kramer, the physical therapist who works with Hart on the trails and at Bryn Mawr Rehab, a rehabilitation hospital near Thorncroft. "The best rehabilitation equipment can only exercise a patient in two-dimensional movement. The horse's walk is a three-dimensional gait like a human being's—forward to back, side to side, and up and down—and it helps Jay's muscles remember exactly how he's supposed to be moving when he's walking. The other benefit is psychological. Jay tried to get out of his physical therapy, but he came to me and asked, 'Can I get in the equestrian therapy program?'"

Equestrian therapy is one of numerous ways animals are helping people recover from injury and disease nowadays. Doctors, nurses, physical therapists, and psychiatrists are increasingly turning to the lower orders to help treat head injuries, Alzheimer's, AIDS, high blood pressure, strokes, movement disorders in arms and legs, broken or injured limbs, even clinical depression.

Not only pet lovers but also respected heart surgeons say, "Get a dog," because it's been proved that owning a dog prolongs a heart-attack survivor's life and lowers cholesterol levels. Elderly people grin as they stroke the bristles of Petunia, a therapy pot-bellied pig owned by a nurse in Philadelphia. Nervous folks awaiting root-canal work stare at fish in the dentist's fish tank—and feel relaxed and calm. Chinchillas, those ultrasoft rodents often killed for fur coats, accomplish what parents and teachers at the Devereux Foundation near Pottstown sometimes can't— turn troubled children into eager students.

An estimated half of the nursing homes in the United States have therapy animal programs because of the brightness and cheer they bring the old, the lonely, and the depressed. Dogs are star visitors at the children's cancer and AIDS wards at the National Institute of Health in Bethesda, Maryland. Animals do their best therapy work with the neediest of all—the very young and old, the abused and frightened, the sickest and loneliest.

"There are many species and many therapy applications for many diseases," says Alan Beck, the pioneering researcher who left the University of Pennsylvania and now heads a Purdue University center that studies the human-animal bond. "But the bottom line is that animals are very effective, very cost-effective replacement family. Especially in hospital and institutional settings, family is hard to come by. People empower their animals with a kind of humanity, uninhibitedly share their love, and accept the animal's version of love in return. All those times when you really need someone to hug, the animal is there for you."

Every week, it seems, scientific research proves new ways animals can improve human health. But according to Beck, "It's been going on throughout human history. The English used farm animals in mental hospitals in the 1500s. Farm animals helped rehabilitate stressed-out World War II fliers in a hospital in New York State. People have intuitively understood that seeing animals—being with animals—restores a sense of normalcy."

"In Victorian England, overly stressed people were advised to take up horseback riding or get a dog," adds The Delta Society's Maureen Fredrickson. "And there was a popular saying, 'The outside of a horse is good for the inside of a man.' "

How Can Birds Lower Cholesterol?

Buy a parrot. Rescue a starling, those birds that cluster on power lines—they make remarkable pets and mimic those who can chant "Defense! Defense!" at the TV, says Meredith West, editor of the journal *Animal Behavior*. Okay, buy a cat, dog, or twenty-foot reticulated python. It doesn't much matter. Owning a pet—any pet—lowers your blood pressure and cholesterol, according to a study of eleven thousand people reported in an Australian medical journal last year, said Philadelphia psychiatrist Aaron Katcher, professor emeritus at the University of Pennsylvania. The study confirmed Katcher's research at Penn ten years ago that showed that stroking an animal lowers your blood pressure.

How Do Rabbits Relieve Pain?

"Rabbits are great with adults in pain-management programs," Maureen Fredrickson says. "People in hospitals who have cancer or heart surgery, there's a lot of anxiety and pain. To have a rabbit come in and sit on your lap and stroke it is very relaxing. It relieves anxiety and stress, reduces blood pressure." Rabbits are increasingly used in nursing homes and in arthritis therapy. Most arthritis patients would much rather groom the fur of an Angora rabbit than do finger exercises, Fredrickson says. "They sit with the rabbit on their lap stroking and plucking the fur," Fredrickson says. "It works the same muscles and is far more pleasurable."

How Do Pets Comfort Heart Patients?

In a study of recovering heart-attack victims by Aaron Katcher at the University of Pennsylvania and James Lynch of the University of Maryland, heart patients with pets had much higher survival rates. Out of fifty-eight people with animals, three died during the control period. Out of twenty-eight people with similar heart conditions and no animals, eleven died. Katcher attributes the higher survival rates to companionship—many studies have shown that people with more companionship live longer than people who live alone—and to reduced stress and lower blood pressure in pet owners.

How Do Pigs Perk Up the Elderly?

Dogs and cats are the most frequent nursing-home visitors, but pigs and rabbits are making inroads. Joan Abrams, a school nurse and part-time maternity nurse at Temple University Hospital in Philadelphia, takes her shar-pei, Mai Ling, and her Vietnamese pot-bellied pig, Petunia, on therapy visits to Children's Hospital of Philadelphia and Chapel Manor Nursing & Rehabilitation Center in Philadelphia. Sometimes Petunia wears a wedding dress. "They love her," Abrams says. "She's a real sweet pig. Animals can do things that nothing else in medicine can do."

Colorado nursing-home residents are occasionally visited by two adult-therapy llamas. "They go into a patient's room," Frederickson says. "And someone who's severely depressed, someone with Alzheimer's who won't even come out of the room, all of a sudden they reach out to pet a llama and start smiling."

How Can Dolphins Cheer Up the Depressed?

At dolphin research centers in Israel, England, and Florida, patients who suffer from Down's syndrome, autism, brain damage, depression, cancer, and other ailments seek relief by swimming with dolphins.

In Israel, former cancer patient Helen Davis, a nurse, credits dolphin therapy with helping her remission. "The first thing I noticed was that they seemed to smile at me," she says. "At the oncology unit, no one smiles; they just wait to die. For the first time in a long while, I saw pure friendship, no pity." When a group of wheelchair-bound children went into the sea, one boy who had been very angry and depressed kissed a dolphin and "was so happy, so proud of himself," Maya Zilber told the *New York Times*. He began to show "warm feelings, signs that he cared about others."

Alan Beck and others are skeptical of therapy wildlife programs because, unlike domesticated animals, the programs "may not be mutually beneficial to the wildlife."

How Can Fish Lower Blood Pressure?

A study at the University of Pennsylvania showed that dental patients who looked at a fish tank for a half hour before dental surgery were significantly more relaxed before the operation. Thanks to the benefits, you can now find aquariums in children's hospitals and other health centers nationwide, says Beck, who led the research at Penn. Although it hasn't been documented, researchers speculate that watching other animals, especially birds, will provide the same sort of therapeutic relaxation response.

How Do Cats Assist Car-Accident Victims?

People recovering from strokes are often assigned to lift light dumbbells to recover strength. "But it's a lot more interesting and motivational to throw a tennis ball for a dog," Maureen Fredrickson says. "The physical therapist isn't saying, 'A little higher, a little higher.' The dog doesn't say, 'Oh, you didn't throw that the right way.' The person is naturally going to try to throw it farther for the dog. It's fun."

Animal therapy is very effective in all sorts of motion-recovery programs, Fredrickson says. For instance, someone recovering from a deep coma, or a car-accident victim, can stroke a cat to regain range of motion in the arm. Children with speech problems practice asking a dog to "fetch" or "sit"—and have lots of fun and no criticism.

How Can Chinchillas Calm the Hyperactive?

At the Devereux Foundation's treatment facility for children with attention deficit disorder and hyperactivity, many of the children, ages nine to fifteen, can't focus on schoolwork. Some suffer a "conduct disorder" that makes them very aggressive and given to outbursts. One boy had to be restrained forty times in six months—until he began to care for a pet guinea pig. Then his behavior improved markedly. Under the direction of Aaron Katcher, the foundation has established a "companionable zoo" of mice, gerbils, chinchillas, rabbits, goats, miniature pigs, and other small animals. Therapy animals.

For the last two years, ninety children have devoted five hours of class time each week to learning about the animals' habitats and behavior—and caring for them. When an animal dies, the children—often from broken homes—support each other in nurturing ways they've never shown.

"We've been able to demonstrate with very objective means a reduction in symptoms, a reduction in aggressive behavior, and increased interest in school," Katcher says.

How Do Big Dogs Reassure Small, Abused Children?

A two- or three-year-old child is only about thirty inches tall—three inches shorter than the shoulder of a 145-pound Irish wolfhound. If the child has been physically abused by parents, there's no better way to put a smile on his face and raise his self-esteem than by letting him walk Gaibhne, the Irish wolfhound, says Maureen Fredrickson, Gaibhne's owner.

If six or seven abused children together pull Gaibhne on one leash, the big dog trails gently along and the children "get a feeling of sharing, the message not to be afraid, not all big things are hurtful. He never scolds, judges. It's a tremendous confidence builder."

How Can Assistance Dogs Save Your Life?

On Maryland's Eastern Shore lives a sweet young female named Perry, an eighty-pound German shepherd who has saved more lives than Wonder Woman. The Eastern Shore is a fine place to watch fireworks, and if you're there on the Fourth of July stop by Centreville and visit Perry, who loves humans and has the same view of us as Saint Augustine: There's good. There's evil. You make the choice and pay the price.

Of course, Perry might be too busy to chat, there in her small house while she's taking care of her handicapped couple. She gets them out of bed, carries them between rooms, brings their medicine, picks up dimes, and saves them from car accidents, house fires, and armed robbers. The last few aren't in Perry's contract, but "Perry has lots of common sense," says her trainer, Winn Strickland, out in the Pennsylvania country where Perry was born. "Can't teach a dog common sense."

Couple summers ago, when she was only one and hadn't met a soul she didn't like, Perry was lying under a picnic table by some woods near a hotel. Tim—that's Tim Bunge, thirty-seven—was sitting on the bench enjoying the evening breeze with Prudence. That's Perry's sister, a black Labrador retriever. Tim learned to enjoy the breeze more after his tractor flipped on the farm and he had four back operations. Sometimes he leans his body on Perry just to walk.

Three dark shapes appeared in the night. They wanted money. "I'm gonna cut you," one said, reaching into his coat pocket. "And I'm gonna cut your dog. It's a Lab and it won't bite." He motioned to Prudence. Perry came around the picnic table and stood with her ears forward, head erect, "and that look in her eye," says Cindy, Tim's wife, "that says, 'Don't even think about it.'"

Tim said, "Go get them!" So Perry and Prudence chased the men fifty yards across a field. The men never came back.

This May, Cindy, who wears a neck brace from a series of car accidents, was about to cross a street in Washington, D.C., when Perry leaped and blocked her path, stopping Cindy cold. A car sped by within two inches of the dog. Cindy hadn't looked left. "That dog saved your life!" a man cried from across the street.

Two days later, Cindy was napping to ease her ceaseless spinal pain, naps that Perry is trained not to disturb. But Perry kept licking Cindy's face, whining in her ear, then whining in front of an electric socket. Cindy got up to look. A plug was melting in the socket. "Another few minutes, this old house would have burned down," the electrician said when he came.

On days when Tim and Cindy are both in constant pain, Tim says God is either playing an absurd joke on them or He's got a plan. Tim prefers to believe in the plan. Cindy says, "Perry and Prudence have given us our dream. To start our own training school for assistance dogs." That's what they were doing in the woods near the hotel, scouting for land for the school.

Cindy knows the numbers: Forty-three million Americans could use an assistance dog, but only ten thousand currently have one because of the price—as high as $10,000—and the years of waiting to find a qualified dog. That's why, on July 4, the Assistance Dog United Campaign will be launched with a $250,000 donation by Pro Plan pet foods in St. Louis, to help folks find dogs like Perry and Prudence.

Perry is not involved in the campaign. She's too busy working in a small house in Maryland. "She's given us our freedom," Cindy says. That's why some folks call them Independence dogs.

CHAPTER 15

DEAR WILD THINGS

IN WHICH WE ANSWER DEFINITIVELY
ALL THE MYSTERIES OF LIFE

"Wild Things" readers ask the most literate questions about important issues affecting our commonweal, such as submissive urination. One could argue that this was not what Thomas Jefferson intended for the First Amendment, but the "Wild Things" staff has been recently flooded with questions from pet lovers whose veterinarians, spouses, and friends *just don't get it*. We're here to help.

Dear "Wild Things":

"How the heck can I break (without breaking body or spirit, please) my three-year-old female miniature dachshund, Grendl's, habit of piddling whenever (a) anyone pets her with a full bladder (the dog, that is), prior to one of her twice- or thrice-daily eliminatory perambulations;

(b) when greeted by a member of the family or a close friend who has been absent for hours or days; or (c) when greeted by a new human acquaintance, especially if it happens to be a man (the little sicko!)."

—*Laurie Macdonell-Sanchez, Miami, Florida*

Dear Laurie:

Grendl is employing the very unpleasant technique of "submissive urination." This makes good sense to Grendl, however. "Grendl is doing everything possible in doggie language to say, 'I am inferior to you!'" notes Pennsylvania veterinarian Michael Moyer. "This is appropriate because when you are a miniature dachshund you are inferior to almost everything." When friends visit, greet them with Grendl out-of-doors (it's not so bad if Grendl messes the grass). To break her of the habit, don't make a fuss when friends visit; in fact, instruct your friends to ignore the dog. Introduce Grendl to actual men twenty minutes later, in a low-key way. "Don't do the high-pitched whiny squeal we humans use when greeting each other," Moyer says.

Dear "Wild Things":

"We have a serious problem and . . . the vet can't tell us what to do. . . . It's self-mutilation of our cat, Steinway. . . . The hair on her rump is almost all gone and so is some from the base of her tail. . . . Please advise. Love. Light. Life."

—*Janet Liedeker, Miami Beach, Florida*

Dear Janet:

It's your lucky day. I called Karen Overall, the famous University of Pennsylvania animal behaviorist, who said the first thing to check for is fleas. Since you indicate in your letter that Steinway doesn't have fleas, the problem is likely to be psychogenic allopecia, the fancy term for your cat being obsessive-compulsive and needing antianxiety drugs. Penn just happens to be conducting a study on such drugs to cure similarly crazy cats, and Overall invites you to join the study through your veterinarian. Write Overall at The Behavior Clinic, Veterinary Hospital of the University of Pennsylvania, 3900 Delancey Street, Philadelphia, Pennsylvania 19104-6010.

Dear "Wild Things":

"Four years ago we became the reluctant owners of a 2½-year-old dwarf chinchilla rabbit named Mush (rhymes with push). . . . Now Mush has become part of our family. . . . My husband may be transferred to San Antonio, Texas, this summer, and the problems of moving Mush have become my biggest concern. My veterinarian hasn't heard of any particular problems with moving rabbits and doesn't seem to understand my concerns."

—*Barbara Tamayo, Miami, Florida*

Dear Barbara:

Your fears are well-founded. Rabbits are extremely sensitive to heat changes and are easily frightened by luggage that goes bump in the flight. Driving a rabbit across the Sun Belt in summertime would be a *nightmare* (you could never leave it in the car for a second). Buy the biggest pet carrier that an airline will allow under your seat (the airline will tell you), and purchase Mush a ticket to fly the friendly skies, usually about $25 for a pet.

Dear "Wild Things":

"My husband and I received a bat house. . . . We live in central San Jose. . . . Before putting the bat house in our backyard, we would like to know if, in fact, there are any bats in the heart of the city. Our gift-giver meant well, but we are skeptical. . . ."

—*Roberta Shields, San Jose, California*

Dear Roberta:

In spring our fancy turns to baseball and bats, which are, sadly, endangered. Forty percent of bat species (the winging kind, not the swinging kind, i.e., Louisville Sluggers and Adirondacks) are hurtling toward extinction because of loss of habitat, according to Bat Conservation International. Bats are not—contrary to myth—rabid, evil vampires that tangle in your hair. They are, in fact, harmless, highly useful critters that can do amazing pet tricks David Letterman never dreamed of, like eating six hundred mosquitoes in sixty seconds. (Reports of bats sucking blood from large mammals are overstated; only one-third of 1 percent of bats suck blood from large mammals, and these large mammals live in Latin America.)

There are definitely bats in your neighborhood, but don't despair if your bat hotel has the occupancy rate of a Hawaii hotel during typhoon season. Like a hotelier, you need to market your audience. True, a recent New York State study concluded bat houses *never, ever work*. But Bob Benson of Bat Conservation International insists they work across the United States with the right management of the many variables that make bats happy, such as temperature ranges and a nearby water source. Benson or Mitch Bell at BCI will be happy to help you. Write BCI, P.O. Box 162603, Austin, Texas 78716. Or call (512) 327-9721.

Dear "Wild Things":

"Do you know of any organization or adoption clinic that places older cats? My wife is a cat lover and she has been feeding stray cats for several years. We now have too many."

—*Gilbert Medina, Morgan Hill, California*

Dear Gilbert:

Reader Kay Bushnell of Palo Alto, California, wrote to "Wild Things" recommending the Best Friends Animal Sanctuary in Kanab, Utah: (801) 644-2001. The place has hundreds of acres and puts kitties in "cat foster homes." *Cat Fancy* magazine has names of other such organizations. But Rachel Lamb of the Humane Society of the United States advises, "See these places for yourself and get references. We're skeptical whether hundreds of animals can be provided for with quality care by just a few staff members. Pets need a human bond."

Dear "Wild Things":

"HELP!!! We are at an impasse. Our daughter, Jaimie, age fourteen, desperately wants a dog so she won't have to come home to an empty house. My husband (although he is allergic to dust, mold, cats, etc.) agrees a dog would be a good companion for her and a watchdog for the family. I am the last holdout. . . . I believe it would be unfair to have a dog when we are all away from home between 7 A.M. and 5 P.M. when Jaimie arrives home from school."

—*Lynn Gelman, Miami, Florida*

Dear Lynn:

It's not ideal, but many well-adjusted dogs happily await their owners from 7 A.M. until even 6 P.M. Your husband may be allergic to dogs, too, warns Bucks County, Pennsylvania, veterinarian Michael Moyer. Have him hang around friends' dogs and pick a breed that he isn't allergic to. Poodles, Portuguese water dogs, and some terrier breeds are billed as hypoallergenic. A smallish dog from the shelter— thirty to forty pounds, max—would be ideal. A cat may be even better for your lifestyle. Consider two purebred cats— the Devon rex and Cornish rex—that are advertised as hypoallergenic.

Dear "Wild Things":

"In your column 'Reptiles as pets: where's the bond?' you failed to note many good reasons why people would choose to own reptiles. Reptiles . . . don't have the potential to damage property that cats and dogs possess, and are thus allowed in many apartment buildings. . . . Reptiles make little (if any) noise to disturb neighbors. Reptiles are ideal for people with allergies to the dander of fur-bearing pets. Finally, while it is true that reptiles don't 'bond' with their owners, this has the benefit that the animal can be left alone . . . and not be neglected emotionally. . . . Reptiles as pets are therefore similar to fish. I doubt you would be as critical of fish owners."

—*David Koehler, Mountain View, California*

Dear David:

You make many excellent points. As Glenn Close says in *The Paper*, "We taint 'em today, we make 'em look good on Saturday. Everyone's happy." I hope you and the many Angry Reptile Owners who have written "Wild Things" are happier now.

Dear "Wild Things": How Can I Help Pets in Disasters?

Many readers ask this. The American Humane Association's Emergency Animal Relief Fund has been working to help animals in disasters for a century, most recently in the Southern California earthquake. The AHA is the official disaster relief agency for animals recognized by the American Red Cross. To make donations, write to the AHA at 63 Inverness Drive East, Englewood, Colorado 80112. In addition, the National Pet Disaster Fund was founded after Hurricane Andrew to provide emergency on-site disaster relief for pets and animals. For more information, write National Pet Disaster Fund, c/o Mellon Bank, P.O. Box 616, Harrisburg, Pennsylvania 17108.

Dear "Wild Things": As the Owner of an Afghan Hound, I'm Upset That It Is Being Called the Dumbest Dog. Should I Be Concerned?

Many alarmed Afghan owners asked this question. Indeed thousands of owners of beloved Afghan hounds are waking up nowadays to disturbing headlines, such as YOUR DOG IS THE DUMBEST DOG IN THE UNITED STATES. On the other hand,

Border collie fanciers are puffed up with Purebred Pride. According to a ranking of dog brainpower in Stanley Coren's book *The Intelligence of Dogs*, the Border is the smartest dog in America, a canine Einstein—Oxford, Princeton, Phi Beta Kibble, the whole bit. The Afghan is, well, a fashion accessory.

Bloodhounds? Beagles? Saint Bernards? Borzois? Yes, well . . . um . . . we understand these are very *nice* dogs with a fine future in technical education. If you're the proud owner of a chow chow, chances are you don't have any MY DOG IS AN HONOR STUDENT AT HARVARD stickers on your Volvo's bumper, either.

Doggie dolts, all of them, according to Coren's ranking of 133 dog breeds.

Cheer up, Afghan owners. Stanley Coren, a psychology professor at the University of British Columbia, has been out of the sun too long. This is the author of *The Left-Hander Syndrome*, which argues that left-handed persons die younger. Now, Coren, who bills himself as "a prize-winning dog trainer and authority on dog intelligence," ranks breeds according to trainability, their ability to learn owner-pleasing behavior. Coren based his rankings on a survey of 208 obedience judges in the United States and Canada. This is telling. American Kennel Club obedience trials measure a dog's ability to comprehend extremely abstract and challenging Western philosophical ideas, such as *Sit*. And, sometimes, *Heel*. Obedience and subservience in *working with human masters* merit A-pluses in this SAT test.

That's why, like the human SAT in past years, it's a culturally biased test. Small wonder the top ten cleverest dogs include the Border collie, poodle, German shepherd, golden retriever, Doberman pinscher, and Labrador retriever. These dogs were bred to work with humans. "A

German shepherd was bred to herd and protect, working with a human master," says New York dog trainer Sarah Wilson, an Answer Person on CompuServe's Dog and Cat Forum. "How can you compare that with an Afghan hound, who was bred, before guns existed, to chase down a gazelle, bring it to ground, and probably kill it for food? And to never stop until it achieved its objective, working independently of its master."

That's why the AKC divides dogs into seven groups: sporting, terrier, and so forth. The terriers, who don't grade highly in Coren's list, were bred to go to ground for rodents or to fight other dogs (the pit bull) and selected to keep on truckin', not to be subservient to human masters. Terriers and Afghans are brilliant at what they're supposed to be smart at.

The top-rated dogs also reflect the most popular dogs in the country. Obedience judges see far more goldens than basenjis (the second-dumbest). And the presence of the notoriously difficult-to-train and aggressive Rottweiler as the ninth most trainable reflects the attempts of Rott lovers to get their dogs into obedience classes and trials and correct the breed's bad image, Wilson says.

Wilson is thrilled that her favorite, the Australian shepherd, ranked forty-second. "This is an incredibly intelligent dog, but the last thing a dog lover wants for its breed is popularity. It ruins the breed."

What about mutts?—the dogs most people own. Coren doesn't include them in his ranking, but says if it looks like a collie, it will tend to think like a collie. Lassie, by the way, ranked sixteenth.

Dear "Wild Things": Which Dogs Have Problems With Gas?

According to a recent survey of dog owners by AkPharma, the ten gassiest dogs, in order, were the German shepherd, mutt, Labrador retriever, boxer, Doberman pinscher, poodle, cocker spaniel, rottweiler, beagle, and Dalmatian. (Yes, scientists have determined that *all* dogs have problems with gas.) Dog gas is caused, says AkPharma's Alan Kligerman, by "a pet's not properly digesting the ingredients in pet food." The Pleasantville, New Jersey, company is marketing a new drop for dog food, CurTail, which it claims prevents dog gas. The CurTail symbol is a skunk.

Dear "Wild Things": How Can I Choose an Effective "Ratter" or "Mouser"?

Stewart F. Martin of Clarksburg, Ohio, offers this tip: Kittens that pull their hind legs up when picked up by the nape of their neck will be hunters. Those whose legs hang limp will not. "My grandmother showed me this many years ago," Martin wrote us. Dear Stewart: There is no scientific evidence for this, which probably means it's true. "It sounds great to me," says Susan McDonough, owner of The Cat Hospital in Philadelphia. "There's a lot of validity to these old wives' tales."

Humankind domesticated the cat to provide this service, and cats are still the world's best rodent Robocops to keep mice down in your kitchen. (The world-record holder killed 12,480 rats in six years in London.) If you're looking for a hunter, don't starve your cat. It's a myth that hungry cats are better hunters. In fact, healthy, well-fed cats are more efficient in the killing fields. And don't worry, if your cat's a vegetarian, it can still be just as good a hunter. (It is less likely to eat what it catches, however.)

Warning: Hunting by cats is no longer considered safe by human activists. Rodents that have ingested poisons can harm your cat. Alas, kittens learn hunting from their mama, and not many mamas bother to teach the old ways. Cats don't hunt as much anymore because they don't have to. We do it for them, serving up canned prey. "My cat's attitude is 'You may now serve my mouse, and I want it stuffed with crabmeat,' " McDonough says.

Dear "Wild Things": Can Dogs Scuba-Dive?

Yes. Benji did it in the movies, for example. But if you try this in your neighborhood, you'll earn mention in the "Wild Things" Stupid Human Trick of the Week category. Duane Folsom of Boynton Beach, Florida, has outfitted his Lab mix, Shadow, "The Scuba-Diving Dog," with a fishbowl-style decompressed-air helmet and the dog dives in the ocean and in pools. Dogs, of course, cannot follow the complex breathing precautions to ward off the bends and other diving dangers. "Don't try this at home," says Rachel Lamb of Humane Society of the United States. "Scuba-diving is very bad for dogs."

Dear "Wild Things": Why Do Dogs Love Disgusting Things?

This question comes from Donna Doerr of Denver, Colorado, who writes: "I have two female (spayed) bassets, one of whom has a habit of rolling in smelly debris of unknown origin that soils her fur. . . . Why does she roll in obnoxious material? I know they are just 'dogs' but it is a puzzling behavior . . . and a disgusting one to clean up the mess!! I know, I just finished cleaning one of them, ugh! I know I can't stop the behavior, but maybe if I understand why they do this it will help somewhat."

Dear Donna:

Your bassets are not the only gross little pets in the world. All dogs are like that. "Wild Things" once visited the closely-guarded Alpo test kitchens in Allentown, Pennsylvania, and learned a secret. The test-kitchen dogs—while enamored of doggie-style beef products flavored and dyed to appeal to the human consumer—*truly loved* an unbearably foul-smelling mixture that Alpo wouldn't dream of selling. Alpo didn't become part of Americana with Ed McMahon saying things like, "Your dogs will love this, but it'll make you vomit just to open the can."

Dogs have always been gross creatures. Every hunter has a story that will make you blanch about what Ol' Blue put away. Every parent knows what some dogs will do to a stray used diaper. One study found that a dog's favorite food is beef, second favorite is *absolutely anything*, third favorite is chicken, etc.

(This isn't really true: Dogs won't eat *absolutely anything*. Dogs won't eat rotten meat, such as old roadkill. Canines have evolved a keen ability to tell with a whiff when potentially lethal bacteria is present—similar but superior to the human skill at turning up the nose at smelly leftovers at the back of the refrigerator.

The main reason dogs will eat gross things is that their ancestors, the wolf, evolved the ability to eat *almost anything* as a scavenger in the wild, sort of like the ability teenagers possess to eat the things at the back of the refrigerator. Partly for this reason, strong odors that are repulsive to humans excite dogs. Most important, dogs "smell" rather than "see" the world.

"For us the world is like half a sphere in front of our eyes," says animal trainer Vicki Hearne, "but for the dog the shape of the world is a function of the wind, and the world takes a different shape every day. Their worldview is dominated by a scent pooled in one direction or another."

Thus, a strong, repulsive smell to us can be a thrilling vista to them, a stunning call to their higher nature. A cat poop, a regular Parthenon! Dogs will also roll in malodorous things to "dress up" in a new scent or sometimes just for a thrill.

Dear "Wild Things": What's the Proper Etiquette When Your Cat Presents You with a Dead Mouse?

"Wild Things" must point out we are *not* Miss Manners, but we often get this question. So, here goes:

Remember: Do not visibly recoil with horror or anger, even if the moment you spy the bloodied rodent, half alive, twitching on the kitchen floor. Instead, exclaim, "Oh, joy! This is a joyous moment!"

You must behave exactly as you did when your human

child spoke his first word. Clap uproariously. Exclaim and grin. Gently stroke your champion behind his ears. Let him rub against your slacks, leaving his scent and fur. Then, when your feline is distracted, place your hand over your mouth, pick up the mouse's tail with a napkin, and race it out to the garbage in a sandwich bag. Wash your hands thoroughly.

Your cat is making a gift of freshly caught prey because he is worried about you. He has never seen such a poor hunter. Although he usually regards you as a pseudo-parent, for the moment he has you pegged differently: You have become his kitten. You don't know how to catch and eat mice and small birds, so she (neutered females are more prone to this motherly instinct) will show you.

Eventually your cat will bring back living prey and demonstrate how to claw and beat it senseless, then demonstrate how to eat without utensils. Finally she will take you along on the hunt. No need to go this far. Just feign great happiness, or your cat will "once again find you incomprehensible," Desmond Morris says. Then get rid of the thing.

Dear "Wild Things": Why Should I Keep My Cat Indoors? Aren't Cats a Natural Part of the Eco-System?

No. The domestic cat is an invading foreign species in the United States. According to researchers from the National Wildlife Federation, the mountain lion was an indigenous North American species, but the domestic cat was imported from Europe centuries ago. Research by British biologist Peter Churcher indicates that household cats snare seventy million small mammals and birds in England each year, and the figures are higher in the United States. Household kitties have been known to wipe out an entire species of songbirds. This is a slaughter Mother Nature can do without. Besides, the Humane Society says it's safer for the cat to keep him indoors, where his life won't be shortened by cars, dogs, or rabid animals.

Dear "Wild Things": Why Does My Cat Try to Cheer Me Up When I'm Depressed?

Several readers have posed this question. One Pennsylvania woman was particularly amazed when her cat—a nasty, biting, scratching beast—was miraculously transformed whenever the woman cried. The cat rubbed against her leg, purring gently, as if to raise her spirits.

This is because cats react dramatically to your change in mood—by meowing, following you around, peeing on the carpet, etc. Cats are keen observers of human behavior, and any change in routine can distress them.

Dear "Wild Things": How Can I Escape a Pack of Wild Dogs?

Anne D. Clark of Naugatuck, Connecticut, asked us this. Anne was enjoying a pleasant wintertime walk along the seashore in Puerto Rico when a pack of slobbering, growling wild dogs began stalking her. There were four to six of them—she was too scared to count. "What I did instinctively was to move slowly backward away, and all the time looking at them," Anne told us.

Dear Anne:

We're glad it worked, but Rachel Lamb advises the opposite: "Never look wild dogs in the eye. It's a statement of hostility." If you can't run inside somewhere, hold your hands and fingers up at your chest, avoid eye contact, and say in a low, firm voice, "Go away!" Don't run. That excites the dreaded *carnivore chase instinct.* If knocked down, don't roll around screaming. As with bears, get in a fetal position and hush up.

Dear "Wild Things":

"How can I set up a pet-sitting business? I love animals, and I would go to a pet's home, visit, sit and talk to them, walk them, give the pet lots of love and attention."

Maria B. Borja, Granbury, Texas

Dear Maria:

Write to Pet-Sitters International, 418 East King Street, King, North Carolina 27021. Or the National Association of Pet-Sitters, 1200 G Street NW, Suite 760, Washington, D.C. 20005.

If you're looking to *hire* a pet-sitter, consider the new Minneapolis-based Pets Are Inn, a national chain with twenty franchise "Ritz hotels for pets." It's a service that places pets in carefully screened private homes where they are "treated as one of the family," the company says. Pets can bring their favorite toys and blankets so it feels like home.

BIBLIOGRAPHY

The author would like to acknowledge the following excellent sources on animals, which he recommends to readers seeking in-depth knowledge on these subjects.

Ellis, Richard and John E. McCosher. *Great White Shark*, New York: HarperCollins, 1991. ($50)

Fair, Jeff. *The Great American Bear*, Minoqua, WI: Northwood Press, 1990. ($39)

Fisher, Helen. *The Anatomy of Love*, New York: W.W. Norton, 1992. ($22.95)

Kelly, Niall. *Presidential Pets*, New York: Abbeville Press, 1992. ($10.95)

Windybank, Susan. *Wild Sex*: *Way Beyond the Birds and the Bees*, New York: St. Martin's Press, 1991. ($10.95)

Winston, Mark L. *Killer Bees*: *The Africanized Honey Bee in America*, Cambridge, MA: Harvard University Press, 1992. ($19.95)

AUTHOR'S NOTE

If you would like to share your own story of caring for an ailing pet, send it to "Wild Things" and we'll use it to help other folks in a future column about properly grieving for a pet. Meanwhile, if you need help right away, contact The Delta Society, Century Building, Third Floor, 321 Burnett Avenue South, Renton, Washington 98055. Or phone Delta at (206) 226-7357 for a list of pet-loss hotlines, support groups, and counselors across the United States and Canada.

INDEX

*I*NDEX

Theobromine, 228
Therapy animals, 236–245
Thomas, Elizabeth Marshall, 68,
    81–83
Thor (Rottweiler), 77
Thurmond, Strom, 93
Tigers, 209
Tigger (Jack Russell terrier), 104
Tillie (elephant), 192
Tkach, John, 183
Tomei, Donny, 236–237
Torre, CharLee, 192
Travel, 87–89, 118–120, 218–
    220
Truman, Bess, 54
Truman, Harry, 24, 54
Trump, Donald, 19
Tufts, Craig, 145, 201–203
Turkeys, 149–152
Turtles, 168–169, 224

Uniforms, dogs and, 71–73

Vietnamese pot-bellied pigs,
    154–156, 239, 242
Viking (German shepherd), 221

Voith, Victoria, 32, 33, 35, 190
Vozobule, Rosemary, 60

Walters, Barbara, 104
War, animals in, 187–189
Washington, George, 50–51, 190
Wayne, John, 110
Wegman, William, 100
Wells, Sue, 146
West, Meredith J., 99
Whales, 185–186, 232–234
Whitney, Wayne, 36
Williams, Michelle, 60
Wills, 220–222
Wilson, Edward O., 146–147, 162,
    198–200, 203–205, 211, 212,
    227
Wilson, Sarah, 4, 79, 107
Windybank, Susan, 12, 13, 15
Wojtek (bear), 188
Wood, Dave, 174

Yuki (mutt), 61

Zeke (spaniel), 23, 58
Zoos, 172–174, 210–211

ABOUT THE AUTHOR

MIKE CAPUZZO is a feature writer and syndicated columnist for the *Philadelphia Inquirer*. His stories have appeared in *Esquire*, *Life*, and *Sports Illustrated*. He has won the National Headliner Award, the Sunday Magazine Editors' Association's top prize, two awards from the National Association of Black Journalists, and has been nominated four times for the Pulitzer Prize. His syndicated humor column, "Wild Things," was awarded the President's Award by the American Society for the Protection of Cruelty to Animals for its "characteristically humorous and respectful stance toward animals."